Student
Solutions Manual

for use with

Practical
Business Statistics

Fourth Edition

Andrew F. Siegel
University of Washington

Irwin
McGraw-Hill

Boston   Burr Ridge, IL   Dubuque, IA   Madison, WI   New York   San Francisco   St. Louis
Bangkok   Bogotá   Caracas   Lisbon   London   Madrid
Mexico City   Milan   New Delhi   Seoul   Singapore   Sydney   Taipei   Toronto

McGraw-Hill Higher Education

A Division of The McGraw·Hill Companies

3 4 5 6 7 8 9 0 BKM/BKM 9 0 9 8 7 6 5 4 3 2 1

ISBN 0-07-233617-X

http://www.mhhe.com

Table of Contents

Chapter 1: Introduction

Defining the Role of Statistics in Business

Odd Problem Solutions

1. Exercise for student.

3. Exercise for student.

5. Exercise for student.

7. Designing the study.

9. Exploring the data.

11. Designing the study.

13. Exploring the data.

15. Hypothesis testing.

Chapter 2: Data Structures

Classifying the Various Types of Data Sets

Odd Problem Solutions

1. Exercise for the student.

3. Exercise for the student.

5. a. Exercise for the student.

    b. Exercise for the student.

7. Multivariate analysis could be used to predict one variable (your profit) based on several others (competitors' performance, state of the economy, and time of year).

9. a. The individual employee is the elementary unit for this data set.

    b. Multivariate.

    c. Salary and years of experience are quantitative. Gender and education are qualitative.

    d. Education is ordinal qualitative because the categories can be put in a meaningful order from least to most education.

    e. Cross-sectional.

11. a. Months are the elementary units.

    b. Bivariate.

    c. Both of these variables are quantitative.

    d. Time-series.

13. Multivariate cross-sectional data. All variables are quantitative. Variables are (a) last year's spending for TV advertising, (b) last year's spending for radio advertising, and (c) last year's spending for newspaper advertising. Elementary units are competitors.

15. a. Bivariate.

    b. Cross-sectional.

17. a. Qualitative.

    b. Ordinal.

19. a.   Products are elementary units.

    b.   Multivariate.

    c.   Cross-sectional.

    d.   Nominal.

    e.   Quantitative.

    f.   Ordinal.

21. Ordinal.

23. a.   Vacuum cleaners are the elementary units.

    b.   Multivariate.

    c.   Quantitative: price and weight. Qualitative: quality and type.

    d.   Quality is ordinal. Type is nominal.

    e.   Cross-sectional.

25. a.   The elementary units are days.

    b.   Multivariate.

    c.   All variables are quantitative.

    d.   No variables are qualitative.

    e.   Time-series.

Chapter 3: Histograms

Looking at the Distribution of the Data

Odd Problem Solutions

1. Approximately normal.

3. Skewed (towards higher values).

5. a. 2 contracts.

    b. 3 contracts.

    c. No, you can only tell that it lost more than 50% of its value but not more than 100%.

    d. 24 contracts.

    e. Skewed with 3 outliers.

7. a.

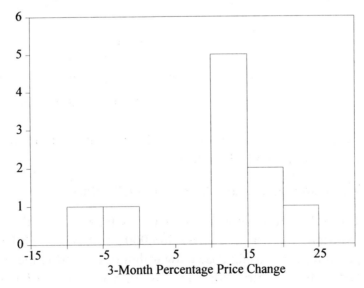

Number of Companies

3-Month Percentage Price Change

b.

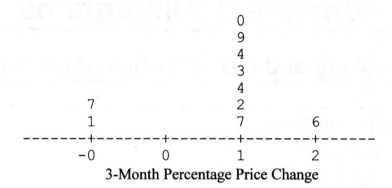

```
                                        0
                                        9
                                        4
                                        3
                                        4
                7                       2
                1                       7              6
       -------+-------+-------+-------+-------+------
            -0       0       1       2
               3-Month Percentage Price Change
```

c.   Shares have appreciated typically by about 10% to 20%.

9.   a.

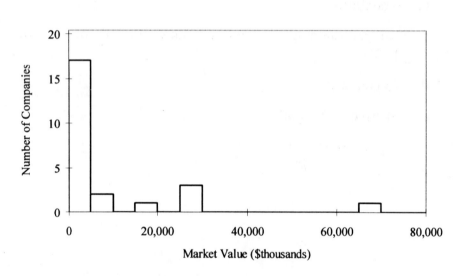

Market Value ($thousands)

b.   Typically, CREF has invested $0 to $30 million in each firm, with one exceptions around $70 million.

c.   The distribution is skewed (toward high values).

d.   The following table gives the base 10 logarithm of the dollar amounts, so that the first number is $\log_{10}(3,463,000) = 6.5395$. Other correct answers are possible, either using base e logarithm or else using the numbers in thousands as given: for the first company listed, you would find $\log_{10}(3,463) = 3.5395$, $\log_e(3,463,000) = 15.0576$, or $\log_e(3,463) = 8.1499$.

Company	Market Value (Thousands)	Log$_{10}$ of Market Value
Australia Gas Light Co	3,463	6.5395
Bed Bath & Beyond, Inc	26,445	7.4223
Best Buy, Inc	1,304	6.1153
Bombay, Inc	1,671	6.2230
Compucom Systems, Inc	71	4.8513
CompUSA, Inc	29,816	7.4744
Egghead.Com, Inc	1,007	6.0030
Ethan Allen Interiors, Inc	335	5.5250
Good Guys, Inc	2,814	6.4493
Heilig Meyers Co	192	5.2833
Inacom Corp	600	5.7782
JD Group Ltd	398	5.5999
Lechters, Inc	293	5.4669
Linens N Things, Inc	315	5.4983
Maxim Group, Inc (the)	706	5.8488
Microage, Inc	52	4.7160
Musicland Stores Corp	2,843	6.4538
Pier 1 Imports, Inc	29,530	7.4703
Rex Stores Corp	2,521	6.4016
Sun Television & Appliances, Inc	416	5.6191
Sunbeam Corp	5,346	6.7280
Tandy Corp	67,305	7.8280
Trans World Entertainment Corp	5,593	6.7476
Williams-Sonoma, Inc	18,822	7.2747

e.

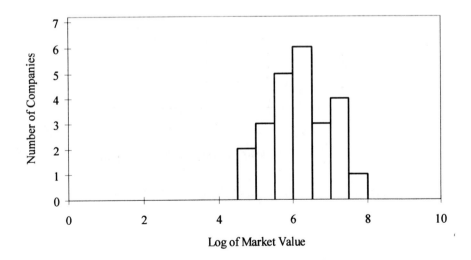

Note that the scale may differ according to the type of logarithm used and whether dollars or thousands are used, but the shape of the distribution will be basically the same in each case.

f.   Approximately normal and fairly symmetric

11.

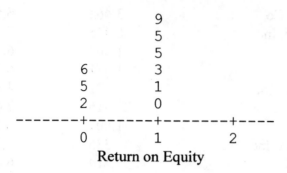

You could also construct the stem-and-leaf histogram with smaller scale for the columns by breaking each column in two. The zeros would go from 0 to 4.9, and the second zero column from 5.0 to 9.9. The tens column would go first from 10 to 14.9, and the second one from 15 to 19.9. It would look like this:

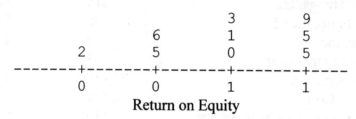

13. a.

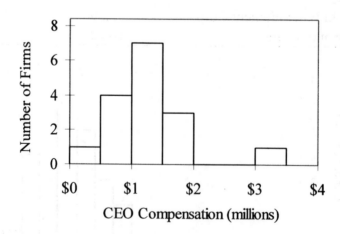

b.   Approximately normal, possibly with an outlier.

15. a.

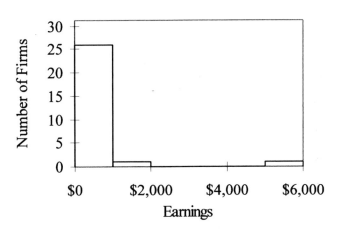

  b.   Skewed with an outlier (possibly two outliers).

17. a.

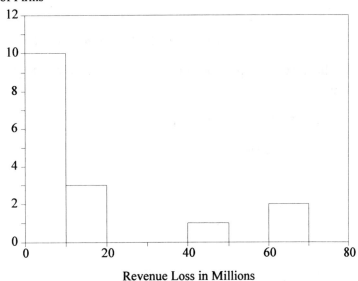

  b.   The distribution is skewed (toward high values), and shows two large gaps with
        three outliers. In particular, 13 of the 16 data values are crammed into the first
        two columns of the display.

19.   a.

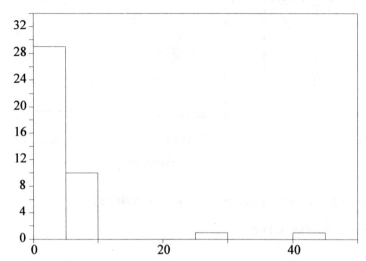

Number of Defective Motors in Each Batch of 250

b.   The distribution is markedly skewed (towards high values), with two extreme outliers.

c.   The outliers are at 25 & 41.

d.

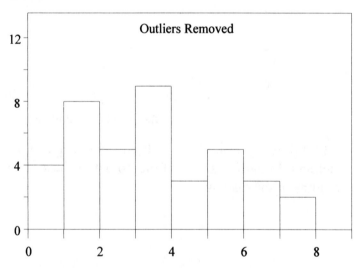

Number of Defective Motors in Each Batch of 250

e.   In two particular batches, a large numbers of motors were rejected for poor quality. Otherwise quality has been approximately normally distributed, extending from about 0 to 8 rejections, and with a typical value approximately 4.

21.

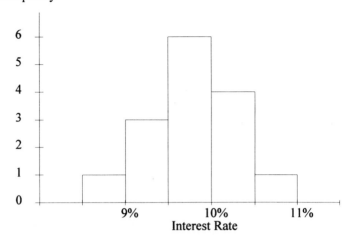

Approximately normal.

23. a.

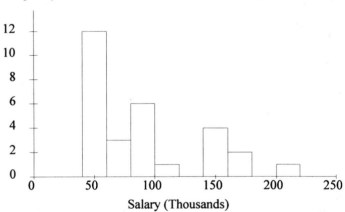

b.   Skewed (towards high values).

c.   Typical salaries were from about $40,000 to about $100,000, with some even higher. The skewness indicates that lower salaries are more likely than higher salaries in general.

25.

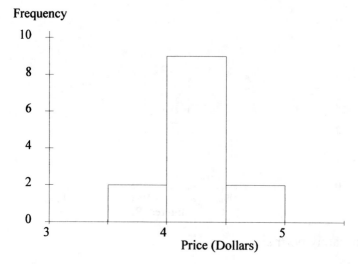

Approximately normal.

27. a.

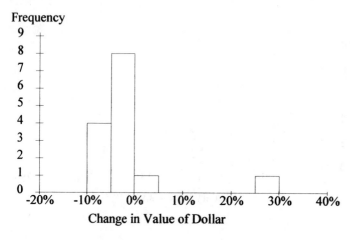

b. Approximately normal with an outlier.

29. a. Here are two possibilities:

```
                      1                3
                      1                3    7    3
                      2    6           1    7    2
          7    0    5  3    9    4      0    5    1
         --+---+---+---+---+---+---+---+---+
         -20  -20  -10  -10  -0   -0    0    0   10
                      Percent Change
```

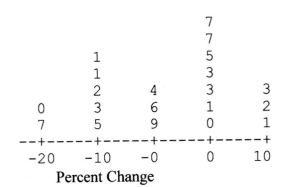

```
                                  7
                                  7
                1                 5
                1                 3
                2       4         3         3
        0       3       6         1         2
        7       5       9         0         1
      --+-----+-----+-----+-----+
        -20     -10     -0        0        10
              Percent Change
```

b.

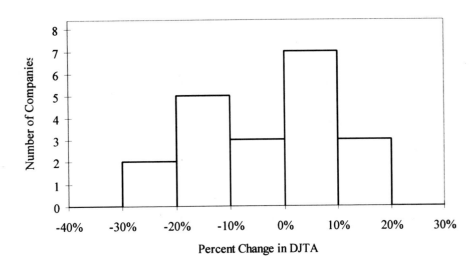

c.   Approximately normal (with randomness).

Chapter 4: Landmark Summaries

Interpreting Typical Values and Percentiles

Odd Problem Solutions

1. a. Average is 15.6 defects per day.

    b. Median is 14 defects per day.

    c.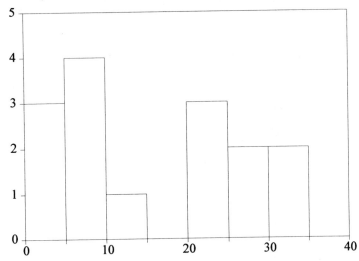
    Number of Days

    Daily Number of Defective Cars

    d. Mode is 7.5 defects per day. (With quantitative data the mode is defined as the value at the highest point of the histogram, perhaps as the midpoint of the highest bar). With a different histogram (different bar widths, for example) a different value of the mode could be found.

    e. Lower quartile is 6, upper quartile is 24.5 defects per day.

    f. Smallest is 0, largest is 34 defects per day.

g.   Number of Defects per Day

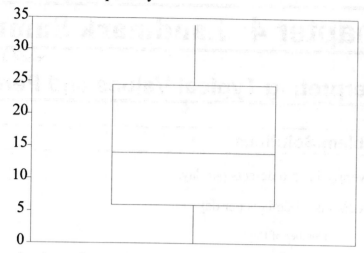

h.   Percent of Total

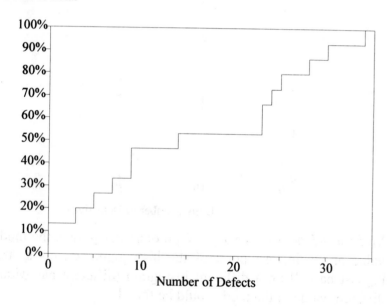

i.   The 90th percentile is 30 defects per day.

j.   The percentile ranking is approximately 87%, as can be seen from the cumulative distribution function, as follows:

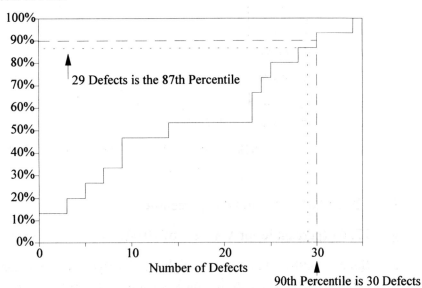

3. a.

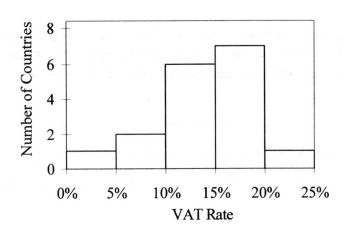

Approximately normal.

b.   14.71% average.

c.   15% median.

d.   They are close to one another, as we expect for an approximately normal distribution.

e.

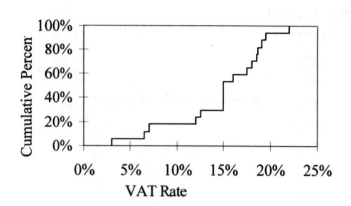

f. 12%, 18.6% (20th and 80th percentiles).

g. 17.7% (percentile for VAT tax of 10%).

5. a. Beta = 0.981. This is a weighted average of the betas (2.4, 0.6, and 1.2) weighted according to the market values (shares times price: 3,500; 17,600, and 7,950).

    b. Selling all shares of Spec. Comp. will realize $35×100 = $3,500. This will buy $3,500/53 = 66 shares of Dependable Conglomerate. Added to the original, gives 216 shares of Dependable Conglomerate. The new portfolio would consist of:

    200 shares Conservative Industries at $88 per share, beta = 0.6

    216 shares Dependable Conglomerate at $53 per share, beta = 1.2

    The beta of this new portfolio, 0.836, has indeed decreased from 0.981.

7. $13.80.

9. Overall market penetration of 19.75%, using a weighted average.

11. Per capita tax burden is $1,607.46, the weighted average per-capita-tax, weighted by population.

13. a. Average loan fee is 1.61%.

    b. Median loan fee is 1.75%.

    c. The mode is 2.00%, with 7 out of the 14 cases having this value. Alternately, the midpoint of the highest bar of a histogram might be used to find a value close to 2%.

    d. It might be argued that the mode is the most useful description of the typical loan fee, since half the banks are charging this amount. However, the mode is also the largest value, an extreme value, and so one of the other summaries might be preferable.

15.   a.   The average is 115.35.

     b.   The median is 100.

     c.

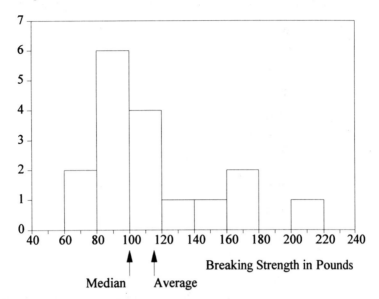

The average and the median are not the same. The average is larger than the median due to skewness of the distribution.

     d.

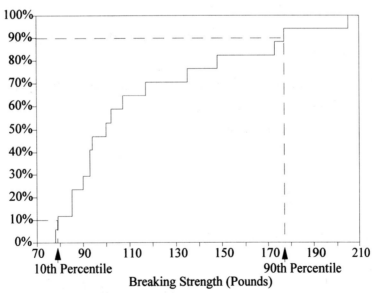

     e.   The 10th percentile is 79 pounds, i.e. 10% have a breaking strength of 79 pounds or less. The 90th percentile is 177 pounds.

     f.   No, these supplies do not qualify. These supplies can provide a breakage value of 100 pounds or more only about 50% of the time. Since management would like the breakage value to be less than 100 pounds a maximum of 10% of the time, you would compare to the 10th percentile. This would need to be at least 100 pounds for these conditions to be met.

17. a.   The average share is 8.19%. The median share is 4.90%.

b.

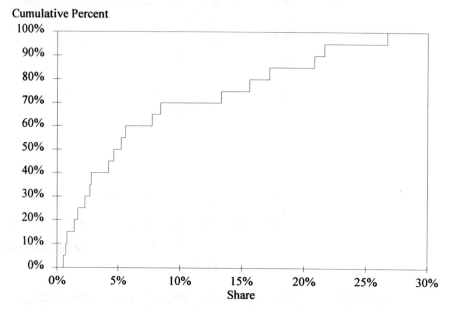

c.   The 80th percentile is 17.2%

19. a.   The average is –1.09%.

b.   On average the dollar weakened (because the average percent change is negative).

c.   The median is –2.80%. The average is higher primarily due to the outlier (Brazil).

d.

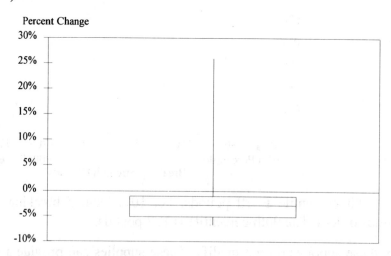

21. a.   The average yield is 5.99%.

b. The median yield is 6.00%.

c. The lower quartile is 5.92%. The upper quartile is 6.08%.

d. The five-number summary is 5.79%, 5.92%, 6.00%, 6.08%, 6.15%.

e.

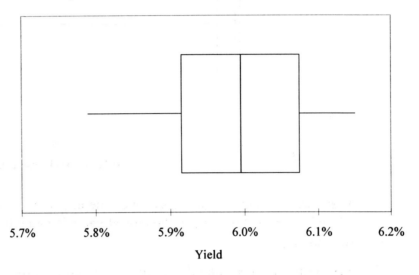

f.

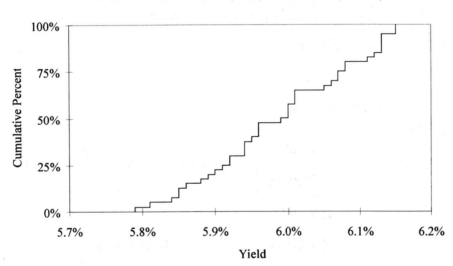

g. 5.90% is the 21st percentile.

h. The 85th percentile is 6.1%.

23. a. The average is $8,410,750.

b. The median is $1,487,500.

c. The average is larger than the median.

d. The five-number summary is $52,000; $366,500; $1,487,500; $5,469,500; $67,305,000.

e.

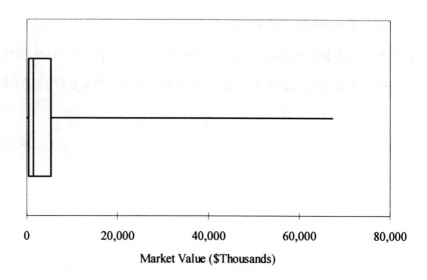

Market Value ($Thousands)

There are two suggestions of skewness here: (1) the median is not at the center of the box and (2) the line to the largest value is much longer than the line to the smallest value.

f. Yes. With skewness like this (with a long tail towards large values) we expect the average to be larger than the median.

25. a. 42.1% (this is 8/19).

b. Law of Desire.

c. They are the same.

27.

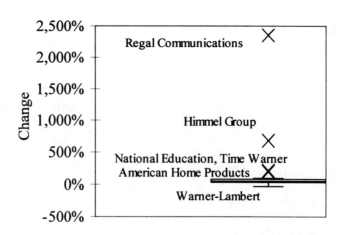

29. a.

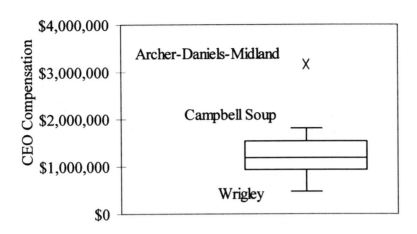

    b. $850,000.

31. a.   The average is 4.39. The median is 3.

    b.   The average is now 2.92. The median is still 3.

    c.   The average is very sensitive to the presence of outliers. Removing them reduced the average value from 4.39 to 2.92; this is a sizable percentage change for the average value. The median is unchanged by the removal of the two outliers. It is quite insensitive to this change.

33. a.   The average is –3.4%.

    b.   The median is –2.25%

    c.   The five number summary is –27.3%, –11.95%, –2.25%, 6.35%, 13.1.

    d.

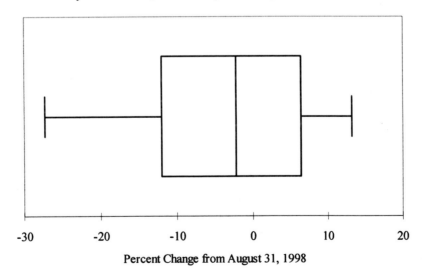

Percent Change from August 31, 1998

e.

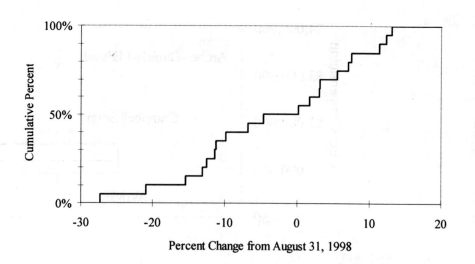

f.   10.00% is the 85th percentile. The 90th percentile is 11.85%

Chapter 5: Variability

Dealing with Diversity

Odd Problem Solutions

1. a. The average budget is $49.50 million.

   b. The standard deviation is 55.75, measured in millions of dollars.

   c. The standard deviation indicates, approximately, how far the individual budget amounts are from their average.

   d. The range is 185, measured in millions of dollars.

   e. The range is the largest minus the smallest. The firm with the largest budget has 185 million more to spend than the firm with the lowest budget.

   f. The coefficient of variation is 1.13. There are no units of measurement, i.e. this is a pure number and will be the same no matter which units are used in the calculation.

   g. A coefficient of variation of 1.13 indicates that the size of the advertising budget for these firms typically varies from the average price by 113% (that is, by 113% of the average).

   h. The variance is 3,108, measured in squared millions of dollars.

   i. There is no simple interpretation because the variance is measured in squared millions of dollars, which are beyond our ordinary business experience.

j.

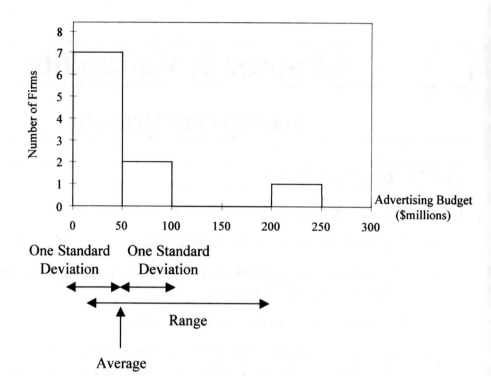

3. a. The average is $49.5 million times the current exchange rate.

    b. The standard deviation is $55.75 million times the current exchange rate.

    c. The range is $185 million times the current exchange rate.

    d. The coefficient of variation, 1.13, does not change because it is the ratio of the average and the standard deviation. Both of these are multiplied by the same value, and these then cancel out.

5. a. Average assets: $10,121 (in millions, as in the data table).

    b. The standard deviation of assets is $7,811 (millions). This summarizes, typically, how different individual funds are from the average of all of them in the list.

    c. There are 38 data values within one standard deviation of the average (between $2,310 and $17,932). Thus 95% of the data values fall within one standard deviation from the average. This is much more than the approximately two-thirds you would expect for a normal distribution.

    d. There are 39 mutual funds within two standard deviations from the average (between −$5,502 and $25,743). Thus 97.5% of data values fall within two standard deviations of the average. This is slightly larger than the 95% you would expect for a normal distribution.

e. There are 39 mutual funds within three standard deviations from the average (between –$13,313 and $33,555). This result, 97.5%, is somewhat less than the 99.7% you would expect for a normal distribution.

f.

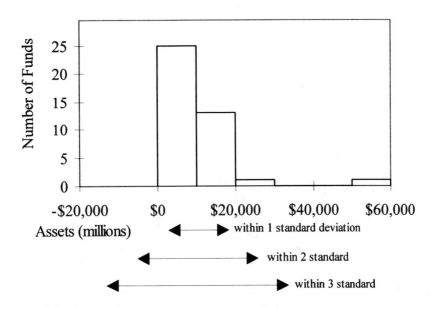

The histogram shows an outlier and some skewness, so the data are not normally distributed. The arrangement of data values within one, two and three standard deviations of the average does not need to agree with what we expect for a normal distribution.

7. With the outlier removed the average diminishes from 10.4 to 9.70. The standard deviation decreases from 7.19 to 5.53. The distribution is approximately normal, although there may be some skewness in the histogram. The percentage within one standard deviation of the average changes from 84.4% to 65.9%, which is closer to the two-thirds expected for a normal distribution.

a. Average number of executives is 9.70.

b. The standard deviation, 5.53, indicates that these firms differ from the average by approximately 5.53 executives.

c. There are 29 corporations (65.9%) within one standard deviation from the average (from 4.17 to 15.23). This is close to the two-thirds expected for a normal distribution.

d. There are 41 corporations (93.2%) within two standard deviations of the average (from –1.36 to 20.77). This is close to the 95% expected for a normal distribution.

e. All 44 corporations (100%) are within three standard deviations of the average (from –6.89 to 26.30). This is close to the 99.7% expected for a normal distribution.

f.

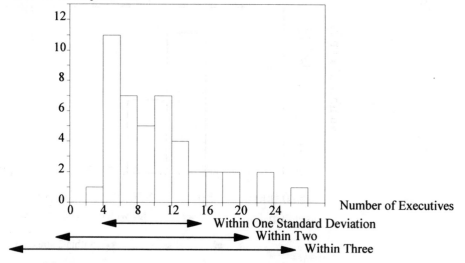

This distribution is approximately normal, although there may be some skewness. Thus it is reasonable that the percentages within one, two, and three standard deviations agree approximately with what is expected for a normal distribution. In particular with the outlier removed, the distribution is more normal and the percentages are more in agreement than before.

9. a. Total cost of the cartridges produced this quarter is:

$\$0.68 \times 80,000 + \$72,000 = \$126,400.$

b. The uncertainty expressed as a standard deviation is:

$\$0.68 \times 25,000 = \$17,000.$

c. Coefficient of variation for number of cartridges produced:

$25,000/80,000 = 31.3\%.$

Coefficient of variation for total cost:

$\$17,000/\$126,400 = 13.4\%.$

The coefficient of variation of the total cost is smaller than that of the coefficient of variation of the number of cartridges produced because the large fixed costs make the variation appear relatively smaller when compared to the larger cost base.

d. This is $(100,000-80,000)/25,000 = 0.8$ standard deviations above the average.

e. This is (200,000–80,000)/25,000 = 4.8 standard deviations above the average. This would indeed be a surprise, because it is not even within three standard deviations from the average and, for a normal distribution, you expect to be within three standard deviations nearly all (99.7%) of the time. However, if you feel that it is not reasonable to assume a normal distribution for the number of cartridges produced, then it might not be such a surprise.

11. a. Average weight before intervention = 1.658.

b. Standard deviation before intervention = 0.0330.

c. Average weight after intervention = 1.663.

d. Standard deviation after intervention = 0.0563.

e. The standard deviation increased after the intervention from 0.0330 to 0.0563. It appears that the intervention has not been successful in reducing the variability in this production process.

13. a. The average is 42.14%; the standard deviation is 253.25%.

b. The risk is very high, as measured by the standard deviation which is several times higher than the average. The average rate of return, 42.14%, is large compared to historical levels of interest rates (imagine a bank account that pays this much!). This high benefit comes only at the cost of substantial risk.

15. a. The standard deviation is 8.098%.

b. Typically, countries differed from their average change in the dollar value by approximately 8.098 percentage points. This measures the risk or diversity of changes in international currency markets.

17. a. The average is $70.333.

b. The standard deviation is $7.442.

c. The price in a typical city differs from their average by about $7.442.

19. a. The standard deviation is $503.00.

b. There is substantial variation in ticket price from one airline to another. The price for a typical airline in this sample was about $503 from the average.

21. a. The average is 23.13. The standard deviation is 14.02. Individuals are approximately 14.02 either above or below the average.

b. This is 14.88 above the average (38–23.125), and is fairly close to one standard deviation.

c. This is 68.88 above the average (92–23.125). This (92) is 4.9 standard deviations away from the average.

    d.   The first new product was typical because it was within one or two standard deviations from the average. The next new product was not typical because it was more than two standard deviations from the average.

23. a.   The average is 7.08%. The standard deviation is 15.69%.

    b.   Individual companies are approximately 15.69 percentage points away from their average.

    c.   The worst performer is 2.26 standard deviations below average.

    d.

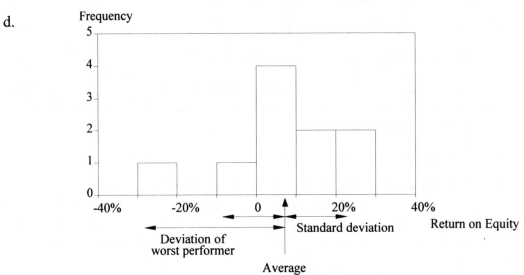

25. The coefficient of variation is 25.4% (or 0.254) both before and after. It does not change because variability has not changed in *relative* terms.

27. The coefficient of variation decreases from 31.3% to 28.1% (or from 0.313 to 0.281) because the (unchanged) variability is now a smaller fraction of the larger average.

29. a.   The standard deviation is 22.1 minutes, indicating about how far from their average a typical movie time is.

    b.   The range is 79 minutes. The longest movie is 79 minutes longer than the shortest movie.

    c.   The longest is 1.50 standard deviations above the average: (136–102.89)/22.123.

31. a.

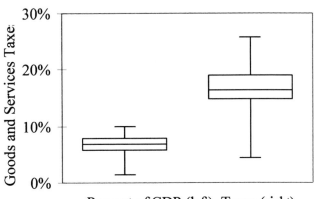

Percent of GDP (left), Taxes (right)

   b. The second variable (on the right) is both larger and more variable than the first
       variable. However, their relative variabilities are similar.

33. The standard deviation is 9.70 percentage points. The range is 33.7 percentage
    points.

35. The standard deviation is $414.06.

37. The standard deviation is 129.08, indicating that your customers typically spend
    approximately $129,080 more or less than the average value.

39. The standard deviation is 0.435 percentage points. The range is 1.00 percentage
    points. The coefficient of variation is 0.271 or 27.1%. These home mortgage
    institutions have fees that are approximately 0.435 percentage points from the
    average fee level. The range indicates the extent from the smallest fee (1%) to the
    largest (2%). The coefficient of variation indicates that the typical loan fee differs
    from the average loan fee by approximately 27.1% of the average.

41. a. The average age is 5.4.

    b. The standard deviation of age is 3.05.

    c. The range for age is 7.

    d. The coefficient of variation for age is 0.565 or 56.5%.

43. a. The standard deviation is 11.6 percentage points.

    b. The range is 40.4 percentage points.

    c. The coefficient of variation is −3.41 or −341%.

Chapter 6: Probability

Understanding Random Situations

Odd Problem Solutions

1. a.   The random experiment is: you wait until the net earnings figure is announced and then observe it.

    b.   The sample space consists of all dollar amounts, including positive, negative, and zero.

    c.   Ford's net earnings for the past quarter.

    d.   The list consists of all dollar amounts that exceed your computed dollar figure:

    Computed figure + .01, computed figure + .02, . . .

    e.   Subjective probability.

3. a.   Wait until the end of the day, then observe the number of seat covers produced.

    b.   The sample space is the list 0, 1, 2, 3, . . . of all possible number of seat covers produced.

    c.   The outcome will tell you the actual number of seat covers produced.

    d.   The qualifying outcomes may be listed as 745, 746, 747, 748, 749, 750, 751, 752, 753, 754, and 755.

    e.   The relative frequency is $8/15 = 0.533$.

5. a.   The probability is $35/118 = 0.297$.

    b.   The probability is $(1-0.297) = 0.703$.

7.   The probability is 0.19. Because the events are independent:

Probability of "A and B" = $0.9 \times 0.9 = 0.81$.

This is the probability of meeting both deadlines. Using the complement rule, the probability that the launch will be delayed due to missing the deadline is 1−0.81=0.19.

9.   a.

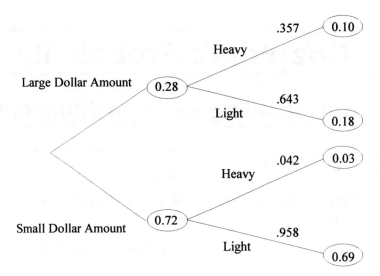

   b.   HEAVY   LIGHT

        LARGE   .10   .18   .28
        SMALL   .03   .69   .72
                     .13   .87   1

   c.

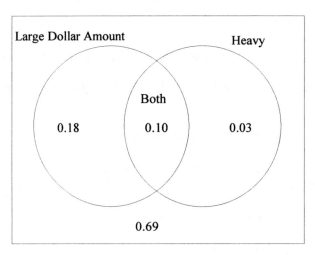

   d.   The probability is 0.31.

   e.   The probability is 0.18.

   f.   35.7% of these are heavy. This is the conditional probability being "heavy" given that these are "large" dollar amount orders

   g.   76.9% are large dollar amounts (.10/.13). This is the conditional probability of being "large", given that they are "heavy".

   h.   No, they are not mutually exclusive because the probability of both events happening, 0.10, is not zero.

i. No, they are not independent because the product of their probabilities (0.28 × 0.13 = 0.0364) is not equal to the probability that both occur (0.10). You can also show that they are not independent by looking at conditional probabilities.

11. a. Let "Good Year" be the first branch and "Dividend" be the second because this is the time-order in which they occur.

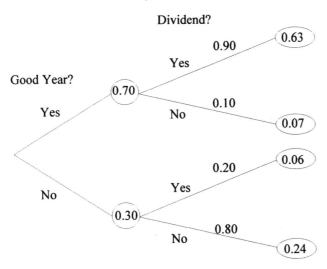

    b. The probability is 0.63.

    c. The probability is 0.63 + 0.06 = 0.69.

    d. The probability is 0.63/0.69 = 0.913.

13. a.

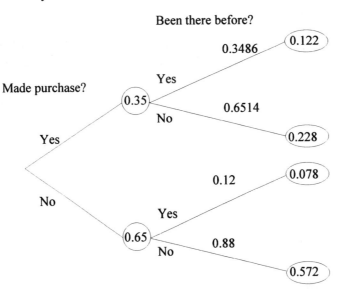

    Alternatively, with the branches in the other order, the result is:

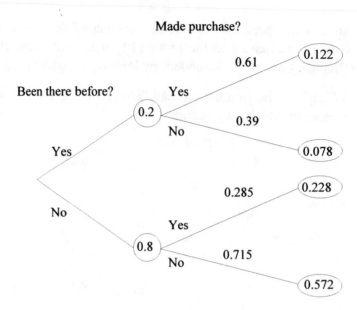

b.   The probability is 0.61.

c.   12.2% of customers.

15. a.   The probability is 0.1955.

b.   The probability is 0.1955+0.0345+0.5645 = 0.7945.

c.   The probability is 0.1955/0.76 = 0.2572.

d.   The probability is 0.7331.

e.   No. They are not mutually exclusive because the probability of both occurring (0.1955) is not zero.

f.   No. They are not independent because the probability of both occurring (0.1955) is not equal to the product of their probabilities (0.23×0.76 = 0.1748).

17. a.

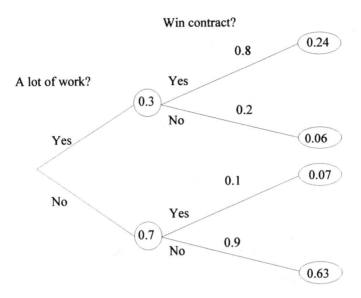

  b.   The probability is 0.24+0.07 = 0.31.

  c.   The probability is 0.24/0.31 = 0.774.

  d.   The probability is 0.06/(0.06+0.63) = 0.087.

19. a.

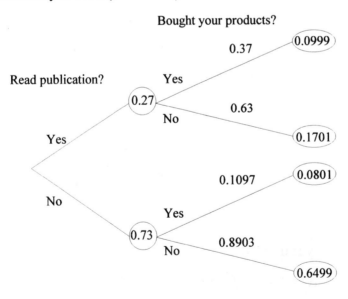

  b.   64.99% of potential customers.

  c.   The probability is 0.0999/0.18 = 0.555.

21. a.   The probability is 0.1/0.75 = 0.1333.

  b.   The probability is 0.05/.15 = 0.3333.

  c.   The probability is 0.05. This represents the fraction of calls that resulted in an "easy" order (i.e., without the need to provide information).

d. They are different because part b (a conditional probability) represents easy orders out of all orders, but part c (an unconditional probability) includes all calls.

e. No. They are not independent because the probability of both (0.1) is not equal to the product of their probabilities (0.75×0.15 = 0.1125). Alternatively, this can be seen by looking at the conditional probabilities.

23. The probability is 0.55/0.6 = 0.9167.

25. a. 2.2% ordered both items.

b. 92.2% ordered neither.

c. 3.96% of those who did not buy the hat did order the mittens.

27. The probability is 0.018/0.116 = 0.155.

29. The probability is 0.68.

31. a.

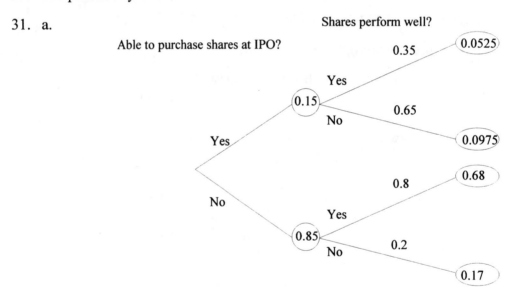

b. The probability is 0.0525.

c. The probability is 0.0525/(0.0525+0.68)=0.072.

d. The probability is 0.0525+0.17=0.2225, or 22.25% of the time.

33. a. The probability is 0.8. This is the complement of the event in part b.

b. The probability is 1/5 = 0.2.

35 a.

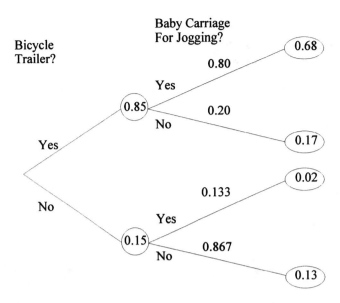

b.   The probability is 0.68.

c.   The probability is 0.13.

d.   The probability is 0.17.

e.   The probability is $0.68 + 0.17 + 0.02 = 0.87$.

Chapter 7: Random Variables

Working with Uncertain Numbers

Odd Problem Solutions

1.   a.   The mean payoff is $8.50.

      b.   The expected option payoff, $8.50, indicates the typical or average value for the random payoff.

      c.   The standard deviation is $10.14.

      d.   This standard deviation, $10.14, gives us a measure of the risk of this investment. It summarizes the approximate difference between the actual (random) payoff and the expected payoff of $8.50.

      e.   The probability is $0.15 + 0.10 = 0.25$.

      f.   The probability is $0.50 + 0.25 + 0.15 = 0.90$.

3.   The risk is $9.17.

5.   a.   The expected loan payment is $37,500.

      b.   The risk (standard deviation) is $16,771.

7.   a.   Mean for apartment = ($130,000×0.6)+($70,000×0.4) = $106,000.

        Mean for single family home = ($100,000×0.60)+($60,000×0.40) = $84,000.

        Mean for selling land = $60,000.

        Mean for casino = ($500,000×0.10)+(0×0.90) = $50,000.

      b.   Standard deviation for selling land = 0.

        Standard deviation for single family home = $19,596.

        Standard deviation for apartment = $29,394.

        Standard deviation for casino = $150,000.

      c.   The gambling casino can be eliminated because it has lower expected payoff and higher risk than selling the land.

d. The decision would have to be made according to the "risk versus return" preferences of the decision maker because, for these remaining projects, higher expected payoffs come with higher risk.

9. a. You expect $0.08 \times 284 = 22.7$ loans, or 8%, to never be repaid.

b. The standard deviation is $\sigma_X = 4.57$, indicating that the number of loans that will never be repaid is approximately 4.57 different from the 22.72 expected.

c. The standard deviation is $\sigma_p = 1.61\%$, indicating that the percentage of loans that will never be repaid is approximately 1.61 percentage points different from the 8% expected.

11. The standard deviation is now $\sigma_p = 1.27\%$. It is smaller, reflecting less uncertainty, because as you move from 50% towards either 100% or 0%, you become more certain about what individuals will do (e.g., near 100% you know that nearly everyone is in favor).

13. The probability is $(1 - 0.20)^8 = 0.168$.

15. a. The binomial distribution.

b. The expected number is $0.86 \times 10 = 8.6$.

c. The standard deviation is $\sigma_X = 1.10$.

d. The expected percentage is 86%.

e. The standard deviation is $\sigma_p = 11.0\%$.

f. The probability is 0.264.

g. The probability is 0.845=0.263910+0.360258+0.221302, found by adding up the binomial probabilities for 8, 9, and 10 customers.

17. The probability is 0.84.

19. a. The probability is 0.58.

b. The probability is 0.31.

c. The probability is 0.11.

21. The probability is 0.05.

23. The probability is 0.67.

25. a. This is a binomial distribution.

b. The expected number is $0.063 \times 2,000 = 126$.

c.   The standard deviation is 10.86563.

d.   The probability is 0.63 of being less than 130. This is based on the mean and standard deviation from parts b and c, then using the normal approximation to find the probability of being less than 129.5 (since normal values between 129 and 129.5 will round to 129).

e.   The probability is 0.69 of being more than 120, using the probability that a normal is more than 120.5 (since normal values between 120 and 120.5 will round to 120).

f.   The probability is 0.91, using the probability that a normal is less than 140.5 (since normal values between 140 and 140.5 will round to 140). Having at least 1,860 working chips out of 2,000 is the same as saying that there were 140 or fewer defects. If you need to be sure you can fill the order, then you will have to increase scheduled production.

g.   The probability is very close to 1. The mean number of defective chips is now $2{,}100 \times 0.063 = 132.3$ and the standard deviation is 11.13396. You now need 240 or fewer defects, and the standardized number to look up in the normal tables is $(240.5-132.3)/11.13396 = 9.72$. This number is off the tables.

27. a. $n = 1{,}000$ and $\pi = 0.53$.

b.   The mean is 530. The standard deviation is 15.7829.

c.   The probability is 0.97.

29. The probability is 0.01 using the normal approximation (mean is 37.5, standard deviation is 5.6458, find probability that normal is more than 50.5).

31. Use $n=1{,}000$ and π from each part of the problem. Use normal approximation to the binomial, probability that the normal is 26.5 or more:

a.   The probability is 0.07 (mean 20, standard deviation 4.4272).

b.   The probability is 0.74 (mean 30, standard deviation 5.3944).

c.   The probability is 0.99 (mean 40, standard deviation 6.1968).

33. a.   This is a Poisson distribution.

b.   The standard deviation is $\sqrt{175} = 13.229$

c.   The probability is 0.21, using the normal approximation (probability of 185.5 or more).

d.   The probability is 0.14 using the normal approximation.

35. a. The probability is 0.037. This is 0.0060967+0.0310934, representing the sum of the probabilities of 0 and 1 contract for a Poisson distribution:
$$e^{-5.1}\left(\frac{5.1^0}{0!}\right)+e^{-5.1}\left(\frac{5.1^1}{1!}\right).$$

    b. The probability is 0.135, computed as $e^{-5.1}\left(\frac{5.1^3}{3!}\right)$

37. a. The probability is 0.377, computed as $1-e^{-3/6.34}$.

    b. The probability is 0.207, computed as $1-(1-e^{-10/6.34})=e^{-10/6.34}$.

    c. The probability is 0.066, computed as $P(X<6)-P(X<5)=$ $(1-e^{-6/6.34})-(1-e^{-5/6.34})$.

39. a. The probability is 0.135, computed as $1-(1-e^{-100,000/50,000})=e^{-100,000/50,000}$.

    b. We expect 9.5% to fail. This is based on the probability of 0.095 computed as $1-e^{-5,000/50,000}$.

Chapter 8: Random Sampling

Planning Ahead for Data Gathering

Odd Problem Solutions

1. a. Unreasonable. This is an unrepresentative sample. The first transmissions of the day might get extra care.

   b. Unreasonable. This sample is unrepresentative and biased, since these transmissions are known to be old, defective, possibly weather damaged and unrepairable. They are not characteristic of the transmissions regularly produced, and certainly not characteristic of "tomorrow's production."

   c. Acceptable, but not good. This is a systematic sample. While you do have information about production throughout the day, you also have all the potential problems of systematic sampling.

   d. Good.

   e. Good. Such a stratified sample would combine random sampling with a closer look at the defective transmissions.

3. Sample d.

5. a. Statistic.

   b. Parameter.

   c. Parameter.

   d. Statistic.

   e. Parameter. Note that this is $\sigma_{\bar{X}} = \sigma/\sqrt{n}$, which involves the population standard deviation and therefore cannot be computed just from sample data.

   f. Statistic.

7. The sample is Illinois Tool Works, Silgan, Newell, and MASCO. (There are 16 firms here; these are numbers 5, 14, 11 and 3 in the list).

9. The sample consists of suppliers numbered 83, 68, 64, and 22.

11. The sample consists of invoices numbered 344, 339, 198, 354, 57, 35, 246, and 26.

13. The standard deviation is $\sigma_{sum} = 10\sqrt{15} = 38.73$.

15. a.   The mean for tomorrow's average, 90, is identical to that of a single machine.

    b.   The standard deviation, $\sigma_{\bar{x}} = 35/\sqrt{40} = 5.534$, is smaller than the standard deviation (35) for a single machine.

    c.   Approximately normal because of the central limit theorem.

    d.   The probability is 0.15.

17. The probability is 0.12.

19. The probability is 0.35. The procedure is to first find the mean (5.55) and standard deviation (6.9676) for individual projects (using material on discrete random variables from Chapter 7), then to use the central limit theorem.

21. a.   The mean is $3,000. The standard deviation is $282.84.

    b.   The mean is $60. The standard deviation is $5.6569.

    c.   That the groups are independent of one another. Alternative answer: that $n = 50$ is large enough to take care of the skewness present.

    d.   The probability is 0.36.

    e.   The probability is 0.45.

23. a.   The mean is 100. The mean of the average is the same as the mean of the individual machines.

    b.   The standard deviation is $15/\sqrt{40} = 2.3717$. It is considerably smaller than the standard deviation for a single machine, 15.

    c.   Approximately normal because of the central limit theorem which states that the distribution of an average of a random sample becomes more and more normal as n gets large.

    d.   The probability is 0.20.

    e.   The probability is 0.79.

25. a.   Using the first word in each firm's name, the 10 samples and their averages are as follows:

First firm	Second firm	Average
Johnson	Avery	2.5%
Johnson	Leggett	5.0%
Johnson	Herman	–3.0%
Johnson	Hon	5.5%
Avery	Leggett	5.5%
Avery	Herman	–2.5%
Avery	Hon	6.0%
Leggett	Herman	0.0%
Leggett	Hon	8.5%
Herman	Hon	0.5%

b.

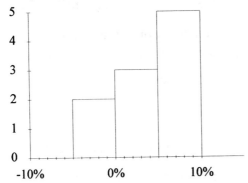

growth rate (averages of two firms)

c.   The sample average is 5.5% for Avery Dennison and Leggett & Platt.

Arranging the digits in groups of 1, because the population has $N = 5$ units, we have: 0 7 8 6 2 7 6 7 3 1. Eliminating numbers larger than 5 or smaller than 1, the first two are firms 2 and 3.

d.

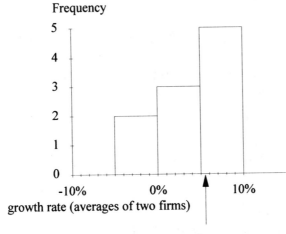

growth rate (averages of two firms)

Average from part c

e.   They are the same because of the definition of the sampling distribution. By "drawing a random sample from the population and finding the average" you first select a random sample, which may be viewed as selecting one entire sample at random from all possible samples. The sample average you compute for this sample is then one sample average chosen at random from all possible sample averages. This is a representation of the sampling distribution.

       For this problem, the random sample chosen in part c selected one number (5.5%, the fifth one) from the sampling distribution of the average as listed in part a.

27. a.   The average, \$499.38, summarizes the typical size of these sales.

    b.   The standard deviation, \$280.70, summarizes the variability of sales by indicating approximately how far they are from average.

    c.   The standard error, \$77.85, indicates approximately how far this average is from the mean of the idealized population of sales made under similar circumstances.

    d.   The forecast is 500×\$499.38 = \$249,692.

29. The standard error is 1.15.

31. The average is \$94. The standard error is $129.0762/\sqrt{10} = \$40.82$.

33. The average is 1.658. The standard error is $0.033023/\sqrt{20} = 0.00738$.

35. a.   The estimated percentage is $p=152/763 = 19.92\%$.

    b.   The standard error is $S_p = \sqrt{.1992(1-.1992)/763} = .0145$ or 1.45%. The sample estimate (19.92%) is approximately 1.45 percentage points away from the unknown population percentage.

37. a.   21/25 = 84% of the sample.

    b.   The standard error is $S_p = \sqrt{.84(1-.84)/25} = 0.0733$ or 7.33%.

39.

Stratum	Population Size	Sample Size	Total Error	Standard Deviation
Large	56	56	\$ 5,018	\$968
Medium	956	143	\$ 2,165	\$152
Small	16,246	325	\$10,792	\$ 73
TOTAL	17,258			

   a.   The sample averages are
         Large accounts: = \$15,018/56 = \$268.1786
         Medium accounts: = \$1,165/143 = \$8.1469
         Small accounts: = \$792/325 = \$2.4369

b. The stratified sample average is
$$(56 \times 268.1786 + 956 \times 8.1469 + 16{,}246 \times 2.4369)/17{,}258 = \$3.62.$$

c. The standard error (without adjustment) is \$0.500:

$$\frac{1}{17{,}258}\sqrt{\frac{56^2 \times 968.62^2}{56} + \frac{956^2 \times 7.12^2}{143} + \frac{16{,}246^2 \times 5.14^2}{325}}$$

The adjusted standard error is \$0.267:

$$\frac{1}{17{,}258}\sqrt{\frac{56(56-56)968.62^2}{56} + \frac{956(956-143)7.12^2}{143} + \frac{16{,}246(16246-325)5.14^2}{325}}$$

The two answers differ primarily because the large accounts (with their large variability) contribute nothing to the adjusted standard error (they have been completely sampled so there is no randomness).

d. The unknown population mean error per account differs from the estimated average error per account (\$3.62) by approximately \$0.267.

Chapter 9: Confidence Intervals

Admitting that Estimates Are Not Exact

Odd Problem Solutions

1. The 95% confidence interval extends from 101.26 to 105.94 bushels per acre (using 1.960 from the t table). (A more exact computer result is from 101.21 to 105.99).

3. The 95% confidence interval extends from $316.42 to $328.46 (using 1.960 from the t table). (A more exact computer result is from 316.27 to 328.61).

5. a. 2.365.   b. 3.499.   c. 5.408.   d. 1.895.

7. a. 1.960.   b. 2.576.   c. 3.291.   d. 1.645.

9. a. 1.740.   b. 2.567.   c. 3.646.   d. 1.333.

11. a. The standard deviation is 15.43.

    b. Approximately one standard error, 5.46.

    c. The 95% confidence interval extends from 23.0 to 48.8 (using 2.365 from the t table).

    d. The 99% confidence interval extends from 16.8 to 55.0 (using 3.499 from the t table).

13. The 95% confidence interval extends from $15.26 to $15.70 (using 1.960 from the t table).

15. The 99.9% confidence interval extends from 54.1% to 73.8% (using 3.291 from the t table).

17. a. $tS_p = (1.960)(0.0135) = 0.0265 = 2.65\%$. Yes, this is less than 3%.

    b. The 95% confidence interval extends from 25.3% to 30.6%.

19. a. The 95% confidence interval extends from $32,511.47 to $42,480.53 (using 2.145 from the t table).

    b. The 99% confidence interval extends from $30,578.08 to $44,413.92 (using 2.977 from the t table).

    c. We are 95% sure that the population mean salary is at least $33,403.81. This is a one-sided confidence interval (using 1.761 from the t table).

21. We are 99% sure that the salary is at least $9,332.61. This is a one-sided prediction interval (using 2.896 from the t table).

23. The 95% confidence interval extends from –0.130% to 0.447% (using 2.093 from the t table).

25. a. The average, 2.34%, summarizes the performance of these stocks.

    b. The standard deviation, 5.98%, summarizes difference from average. The performance of a typical stock in this list differed from the average value by about 5.98%.

    c. The standard error, $5.979817/\sqrt{10}$ = 1.89%, indicates the approximate difference (in percentage points) between the average (2.34%) and the unknown mean for the (idealized) population of similar brokerage firms.

    d. The 95% confidence interval extends from –1.94% to 6.62% (using 2.262 from the t table).

    e. The 90% confidence interval extends from –1.13% to 5.81% (using 1.833 from the t table). The 90% two-sided confidence interval is smaller than the 95% two-sided confidence interval.

    f. We are 99% sure that the mean performance of the population of stocks is at least –2.99% (using 2.821 from the t table).

    g. No, you must either use the same one side regardless of the data, or else use the two-sided interval. Otherwise you may not have the 99% confidence that you claim.

27. The 95% confidence interval extends from $2.27 to $2.41 (using 1.960 from the t table).

29. a. The standard deviation, 2.67, indicates approximately how different individual coils are from the average length of 101.37 meters.

    b. Standard error = $2.67/\sqrt{93}$ = 0.2769. The standard error estimates approximately how far the sample average is from the population mean. The standard deviation (from part a) measures the variability of the individual data values; the standard error estimates the variability of the sample average itself.

    c. The 95% confidence interval extends from 100.83 to 101.91 meters (using 1.960 from the t table). We are 95% certain that the mean length of coils of sheet steel being produced (from which the sample was obtained) is between 100.83 meters and 101.91 meters. (A more exact computer result is from 100.82 to 101.92).

    d. The 95% prediction interval extends from 96.11 to 106.63 meters (using 1.960 from the t table and 2.6843 as the standard error for prediction). (A more exact computer result is from 96.04 to 106.70).

The prediction interval indicates that you are 95% certain the next coil produced will have a length between 96.11 and 106.63 meters.

The prediction interval tells about the length of the next coil produced. It is so much larger than the confidence interval because the prediction interval combines the uncertainty of individuals in the population (as measured by the standard deviation S) with the uncertainty of the sample average (as measured by $S/\sqrt{n}$). The confidence interval in part c is for the population mean, not for a new individual.

e. Yes. A one-sided interval will give you exactly this kind of information. You are interested only in the coils being at least a certain length. There would be difficulty only if you were interested in both sides of the interval.

f. We are 99% sure that the mean length of coils produced will be at least 100.73 meters (using 2.326 from the t table). This is a statement about the population mean, not about an individual coil. (A more exact computer result is at least 100.71).

g. We are 99% sure that the next coil produced will be at least 95.13 meters (using 2.326 from the t table and 2.684316 as the standard error for prediction). (A more exact computer result is at least 95.01).

31. a. $n = 13$, $\overline{X} = 3.2846\%$, $S = 8.1739\%$, $S_{\overline{X}} = 2.2670\%$.

Exercise for student.

b. The population is the rate of return of "all" samples which could be drawn from this mine. The population mean is the average of this quantity, and is an unknown value. The population and population mean are important to the mine owners because they hold the key to the profitability of the venture. If the population mean is at a high rate of return this could be a worthwhile project to undertake.

c. We are 99% sure that the mean rate of return will be at least –2.79% [this is 3.2846–(2.681)(2.2670)]. There is a real possibility that the project will not be economically viable.

d. Based on current information, we cannot be assured of any profit at all on this project. Although the average rate of return is 3.3%, an overall loss is also possible as we continue operations. We should consider abandoning the project. In any case, further testing might be done before development is considered further.

33. a. The idealized population represented by this sample is made up of the typical customers who place orders with you under current circumstances.

b. No. One of the conditions for the validity of a confidence interval is that the distribution be normally distributed. This condition is not met here; the central limit theorem will not help due to the small sample size.

c. The 95% confidence interval extends from $2,790 to $4,774 (using 2.306 as the *t* value).

We are 95% sure that the average sales contract you might expect to land would be for between $2,790 and $4,774. This result depends on the continuation of the population mix of high-order and low-order customers. If this population were to change considerably, e.g. due to marketing efforts, future results might well be different.

d. We are 90% confident that the next contract will have a sales price between $1,253 and $6,311 (using 1.860 as the *t* value and $1,359.78 as the standard error for prediction).

35. The 95% confidence interval extends from $1.67 to $186.33 (using 2.262 from the *t* table).

37. The 99.9% confidence interval extends from 1.629 to 1.687 ounces (using 3.883 from the *t* table).

39. The 95% confidence interval extends from 80.2% to 92.1% (using 1.960 from the *t* table).

41. a. We are 99% confident that the population mean caffeine content is at least 81.47 milligrams (using 2.718 from the *t* table).

b. We are 99% confident that the next cup of coffee will have at least 41.09 milligrams of caffeine (using 2.718 from the *t* table and 20.559 as the standard error for prediction).

Chapter 10: Hypothesis Testing

Deciding between Reality and Coincidence

Odd Problem Solutions

1. a. The null hypothesis, H_0: μ = 43.1, claims that the population mean age of customers is the same as that for the general population in town. The research hypothesis, H_1: $\mu \neq 43.1$, claims that they are different.

    b. Reject H_0 and accept H_1. The average customer age is significantly different from the general population. The 95% confidence interval extends from 29.11 to 38.09 (using 1.960 from the t table), and does not include the reference value (43.1). The t statistic is –4.15. (A more exact computer confidence interval is from 29.00 to 38.20).

3. a. The null hypothesis, H_0: μ = 56, claims that the population viscosity is equal to the reference value. The research hypothesis, H_1: $\mu \neq 56$, claims that it is different.

    b. Accept H_0 as a reasonable possibility. The viscosity of the system is not significantly different from 56. The 95% confidence interval extends from 44.29 to 58.15 (using 2.179 from the t table) and includes the reference value (56.00). The t statistic is –1.50.

    c. Accept H_0 as a reasonable possibility. The viscosity of the system is not significantly different from 56. The 99% confidence interval extends from 41.51 to 60.93 (using 3.055 from the t table) and includes the reference value (56.00). The t statistic is –1.50.

    d. $p > 0.05$.

5. a. The null hypothesis, H_0: μ = 0, claims that there is no difference, on average, in the population "before" and "after" values. The research hypothesis, H_1: $\mu \neq 0$, claims that there is a difference.

    b. Reject H_0 and accept H_1. The observed differences are significant. The 95% confidence interval for the difference extends from 0.03 to 0.41 (using 1.960 from the t table). The t statistic is 2.24.

    c. Accept H_0. The observed differences are not significant at the 1% test level. The 99% confidence interval for the difference extends from –0.03 to 0.47 (using

2.576 from the t table). The t statistic is 2.24. (A more exact computer confidence interval is from –0.04 to 0.48).

d. $p < 0.05$.

7.   a. $p = 15.59\%$.

b. $S_p = 1.347\%$.

c. $(13,916)(0.1559) = 2,169$ dissatisfied customers.

d.   The 95% confidence interval extends from 12.9% to 18.2% (using 1.960 from the t table).

e.   No. The observed percentage (15.59%) is significantly higher than 10%. The reference value (10%) is not in the confidence interval from part d. The t statistic is $(0.1559 – 0.10)/0.01347 = 4.15$.

9.   a.   The 95% confidence interval extends from 0.998 to 1.045 pounds (using 2.201 from the t table).

b. $\mu_0 = 1$ pound.

c.   The hypotheses are $H_0: \mu = 1$ and $H_1: \mu \neq 1$.

d.   Accept H_0 as a reasonable possibility. The observed average weight (1.022 pounds) is not significantly different from 1 pound because the confidence interval (from part a) includes 1. The t statistic is 2.02.

e.   Type II error.

11. a. $\mu_0 = \$20.00$.

b.   The null hypothesis, $H_0: \mu = \$20.00$, claims that the poulation, on average, would indicate $20.00. The research hypothesis, $H_1: \mu \neq \$20.00$, claims that the population mean is different.

c.   Reject H_0 and accept H_1. The 95% confidence interval extends from 17.81 to 18.47 (using 1.960 from the t table). The t statistic is –11.08. The amount consumers would be willing to pay is significantly different from $20.00.

d.   Reject H_0 and accept H_1. The 99% confidence interval extends from 17.71 to 18.57 (using 2.576 from the t table). The t statistic is –11.08. The amount consumers would be willing to pay is highly significantly different from $20.00. (A more exact computer confidence interval is from 17.70 to 18.58).

e. $p < 0.001$.

13. a.   Yes. The observed percentage (52.66%) is larger than 50%.

    b.   No. The observed percentage is not significantly different from 50%. The 95% confidence interval extends from 49.22% to 56.10% (using 1.960 from the t table). The t statistic is 1.51.

15. a.   Because only one side is of interest here. Either we find evidence that the demand is high enough or we don't.

    b.   The null hypothesis, $H_0: \pi \le 0.10$, claims that the population percentage is 10% or less. The research hypothesis, $H_1: \pi > 0.10$, claims that it exceeds 10%.

    c.   Reject H_0 and accept H_1. Significantly more than 10% say they are willing to try your new product. We are 95% confident that more than 10.2% in the population would be willing (using 1.645 from the t table). The confidence interval does not include the reference value (10%). The t statistic is 1.78.

    d.   Accept H_0 as a reasonable possibility at level 0.01. We are 99% confident that more than 9.2% in the population would be willing (using 2.236 from the t table). This confidence interval does include the reference value (10%).

    e. $p < 0.05$.

17. a.   Today's average is 14.34 ounces.

    b.   Yesterday's standard deviation is 0.31.

    c.   The 95% confidence interval extends from 14.23 to 14.45 (using 2.228 from the t table).

    d.   The hypotheses are $H_0: \mu = 14.5$ and $H_1: \mu \ne 14.5$.

    e.   Yes, the difference between the claimed weight (14.5 ounces) and today's observed average (14.34) is significant. The 95% confidence interval does not include 14.5. The t statistic is –3.22.

19. a. $\overline{X} = 208.25$ calories.

    b. $S_{\overline{X}} = 3.17453$.

    c.   The 99% confidence interval extends from 198.39 to 218.11 calories (using 3.106 from the t table).

    d.   Yes, there is a significant difference. The 95% confidence interval extends from 201.26 to 215.24 calories (using 2.201 from the t table) and does not include the claimed amount (200). The t statistic is 2.60. Part c shows that this difference is not highly significant.

21. No. The 95% confidence interval extends from 73.95 to 92.55 (using 2.201 from the t table) and includes 80. The t statistic is 0.77.

23. No, it is not in control. The average weight, 0.2347, is very highly significantly different from 0.20. The 99.9% confidence interval extends from 0.210 to 0.259 (using 4.073 from the t table) and does not include 0.20. The t statistic is 5.83.

25. a.   The null hypothesis is H_0: $\pi = 0.50$. The null hypothesis claims that your favorite candidate will have exactly 50% of the votes. This 50% is chosen because if this were achieved it would result in a tie, not a win. More than 50% is needed for the candidate to be successful.

   The research hypothesis is H_1: $\pi \neq 0.50$. The research hypothesis claims that the vote for your candidate will not be 50%. It will be larger or smaller, but not exactly 50%.

   b.   Accept the null hypothesis as a reasonable possibility. The 95% confidence interval extends from 49.3% to 54.9% (using 1.960 as the t table value) and includes the reference value (50%). The t statistic is 1.48.

   c.   The hypothesis test indicates that, while your candidate got 52.1% of the votes in the poll, this showing is not significantly different from getting just half of the total vote. This is not enough for winning. The result is inconclusive at the 5% level, as far as predicting a victory or not is concerned. Although the sample proportion is larger than 50%, this could be due merely to the randomness of sampling rather than to any advantage the candidate has.

   d.   Reject the null hypothesis and accept the research hypothesis. The 95% confidence interval extends from 55.6% to 61.0% and does not include the reference value (50%). The t statistic is 5.92.

   We accept the research hypothesis which states that the (unknown) population mean proportion is not equal to the reference value of 50%. Since the sample proportion, which represents the population proportion, is larger than 50%, the one-sided conclusion is that your candidate has significantly more than 50% of the votes.

   If your candidate, in fact, had exactly 50% of the vote, you would see such a large percentage (58.3%) only very rarely (less than 1 time in 1,000, since it is very highly significant). This provides strong evidence against the null hypothesis and so we rejected it.

   Any careful statement would have to note that the conclusion tells you about the percentage of people who would have said that they are in favor of your candidate. It does not tell about what they will actually do when they vote.

   e.   The possible outcomes for a two-sided test are:

   (1) The reference value might fall within the confidence interval. You would then accept the null hypothesis and there would be no significant difference between the reference value $\pi_0 = 50\%$ and the percentage found by polling.

This occurred in the first part of this problem. It let you know that the difference in value between the sample average and the reference value is not large enough to establish that your candidate is winning.

(2) The reference value might fall outside the confidence interval, with the reference value smaller than the sample proportion, $\pi_0 < p$. You reject the null hypothesis and accept the research hypothesis, noting that the sample proportion is significantly larger than the reference value.

This is the situation in the second part of this problem. With this result in a two-sided confidence interval you know that there is a comfortable margin of votes in the candidate's favor.

(3) The reference value might be outside the confidence interval, and the reference value might be larger than the sample proportion, $\pi_0 > \pi$. When this happens you would reject the null hypothesis and accept the research hypothesis, reporting that the sample proportion is significantly smaller than the reference value π_0.

If this had happened you would decide that your candidate didn't have enough votes to be elected.

A one-sided test would tell you if your candidate's majority was at least as large as (or as small as) a given value, but you wouldn't have the advantage of some measure of the other side. In fact, both sides are important here. To know that you are significantly winning is very reassuring. But it is also important to know if you are significantly losing because you would probably want to change some things about the campaign!

27. a.   The hypotheses are $H_0 : \pi \geq 0.25$ and $H_1 : \pi < 0.25$.

Accept H_0 because the reference value (25%) is in the confidence interval. We are 95% confident that at least 15.8% of supermarket shoppers are aware of your brand name (using 1.645 from the t table). The t statistic is -1.11 and $t_{statistic} \geq -t_{table}$.

b.   The hypotheses are $H_0 : \pi = 0.25$ and $H_1 : \pi \neq 0.25$.

Accept H_0 because the reference value is in the 95% confidence interval from 14.7% to 27.9% (using 1.960 from the t table). The t statistic is -1.11.

The observed percentage (21.3%) is not significantly different from the goal of 25%.

c.   You accepted the null hypothesis, determining that the result is not statistically significant. Accepting the null hypothesis is a weak conclusion. The results are inconclusive. You know the range which contains the population percentage, but not its exact position. It might be between 14.7% and 24.99999%, or between 25.00001% and 27.9%. There is no way of finding this out using the data currently available. You might have made a Type II error.

The implications for your marketing strategy: It may actually be working. You have many options including (a) conducting a new survey with more interviews in order to obtain a more precise estimate of brand-name recognition, (b) modifying the marketing campaign in an effort to further increase recognition.

29. a. $p < 0.001$. The t statistic is 15.33 and $t_{statistic} > t_{table}$. We are 99.9% confident that the mean weight is at least 24.184 ounces (using 3.090 from the t table) and this interval does not contain the reference value 24. (A more exact computer confidence interval claims at least 24.182).

  b. The system is working. Based on these 100 measurements, we are 99.9% sure that the mean weight per package being produced currently is at least 24.184 ounces. In particular, we are well assured that this is above the 24 ounces we require.

  c. The conclusion of accepting the research hypothesis is a strong conclusion. We have rejected the null hypothesis because there is convincing evidence against it. The difference between the observed weight (24.23) and the reference value (24) cannot reasonably be explained as random fluctuations because the standard error is so small (0.015).

31. a. No, these funds could not reasonably represent a random sample of all mutual funds. The 95% confidence interval extends from 9.89 to 23.67 (using 2.201 from the t table). Since this does not include the reference value (9.41) we accept the research hypothesis. The difference between these funds and all mutual funds is significant. The t statistic is $(16.78–9.41)/3.128865 = 2.36$.

  b. $p < 0.05$. The result is significant, but not highly significant. To see that we do not have $p < 0.01$, note that the t table value, 3.106, exceeds the t statistic of 2.36. The 99% confidence interval includes the reference value.

  c. The hypotheses are $H_0: \mu = 9.41\%$ and $H_1: \mu \neq 9.41\%$.

The assumptions are that the data set is a random sample from the population of interest and that this population is normally distributed. We are assuming that the data are a random sample from the idealized population of mutual funds of this type.

  d. These assumptions may not be realistic. Since some of these funds are part of the same group, the independence assumption of random sampling may be violated. Rather than bringing new independent information to the data set, the information contributed by a group of such funds may be less than the information assumed by the hypothesis test.

e.   The results should be viewed with caution. If performance numbers were totally random and otherwise the same from one fund to another, when these are made into groups (e.g., socially aware funds, international funds, gold funds, high-technology funds, etc.) some will perform better than others. Even if the differences are random, because so many funds are involved, the best fund may appear to be significantly better than the others if it is tested as though it were the only fund being examined (instead of adjusting for the fact that it is the "best" one being tested). The result could be that each year a different random group is declared especially good when, in fact, this could happen even if the results are random. The basic problem is that when multiple groups are tested, the 5% type I error rate no longer applies overall.

33. a.   The idealized population is the collection of all brokers similar to those in the area.

     The null hypotheses claims that your broker's rate of return (the new observation) comes from the same normally distributed population as the sample of brokers. The research hypothesis claims that it does not.

     You are testing against a new observation.

b.   Standard error for prediction $= S\sqrt{1+1/n} = 3.2\sqrt{1+1/25} = 3.263372$.

c.   We are 95% confident that a new observation (drawn from the same population as the sample) will be between 8.46 and 21.93 (using 2.064 from the t table).

d.   Yes, your broker's performance (18.3%) exceeded the average performance of the group (15.2%).

e.   No. This difference is not statistically significant.

f.   The t statistic is $(18.3-15.2)/3.263372 = 0.95$. The t table value is 2.064. This test is not significant ($p > 0.05$). This can also be seen from the fact that the reference value (18.3) is in the prediction interval (8.46 to 21.93) from part c.

35. a.   The term "highly statistically significant" indicates that the productivity values found before and after ownership changes are significant at the 1% level, but not at the 0.1% level, giving a p-value of $p < 0.01$. That is, the observed productivity differences are unlikely to have arisen from random chance alone.

b.   The hypotheses are $H_0: \mu_1 = \mu_2$ and $H_1: \mu_1 \neq \mu_2$. The null hypothesis claims that there is no difference in mean productivity level between firms that are changing ownership (at the time of the change) and firms that are not changing ownership. The research hypothesis claims that there is a difference.

     There are two samples. One is of firms that changed ownership, the other is of firms that did not.

     A two-sample unpaired t test is performed.

The assumptions made are that, first, each of the samples being measured is a random sample selected from its population. Next, each sample average is assumed to be approximately normally distributed. In addition, for the small-sample case it would also be assumed that the standard deviations are equal in the two populations.

c. Reject H_0 and accept H_1. The observed productivity difference is very highly significant ($p < 0.001$) because the t statistic exceeds the t table value 3.291 for testing at the 0.001 level (assuming a large enough sample).

d. They have gained knowledge about the populations their samples were drawn from. The results obtained with statistical hypothesis testing can be extrapolated to the general population of firms changing ownership.

The description of the productivity differences, namely a decline of 3.9%, does not lead to an understanding of whether this number is systematic or could be due merely to random chance causes. With just the description you can't answer the questions: Could it have occurred by chance? Is it within the range of the randomness of the sample? Is it a significant change?

Knowing the t statistic removes much of this uncertainty. You know that this result could have been wrong less than one time in one-thousand repetitions of the tests, had there been no difference. In short, they have generalized from these particular firms to a general statement about how changes in ownership relate to changes in productivity.

37. a. This is a paired situation because each expert contributes two scores, establishing the pairing.

   b. The average for Chardonnay is 18.61. The average for Cabernet Sauvignon is 18.44. The average difference is 0.17.

   c. The standard error is $1.584684/\sqrt{10} = 0.501121$.

   d. The two-sided 95% confidence interval for the difference extends from –0.96 to 1.30.

   e. The observed difference is not significant ($p > 0.05$). This is because the reference value 0 (indicating no difference) is within the confidence interval. The t statistic is $0.17/0.501121 = 0.34$.

   f. A sample of ten experts rated two wines. The average rating was 18.61 for the Chardonnay and 18.44 for the Cabernet Sauvignon. You would like to generalize beyond these particular ten experts to the idealized population of expert testers in general. In particular, you wonder whether the Cabernet Sauvignon would still have the higher mean score for this larger population of experts. This is inconclusive. It is reasonably possible that the mean difference could be zero, and that the apparent superiority of the Cabernet Sauvignon could be due to random sampling rather than to a systematic preference by experts in general.

39. Prices in the Laurelhurst are significantly higher than in other neighborhoods, based on a two-sample unpaired t test. We are 95% confident that Laurelhurst costs at least $33.98 more on average (using 1.771 from the t table and 46.5306 as the small-sample standard error of the difference). The t statistic is 2.50 and $t_{statistic} > t_{table}$.

41. a. The defect rate would decrease by 0.024, estimated.

    b. The large-sample standard error of the difference is $S_{(\bar{X}_2 - \bar{X}_1)} = 0.012219$.

    c. The hypotheses are $H_0: \mu_{new} \geq \mu_{old}$ and $H_1: \mu_{new} < \mu_{old}$.

    d. We are 95% confident that the population mean decrease is at least 0.0039.

    e. Yes. The one-sided test shows that the improvement is significant.

43. a. This is an unpaired situation. There is no natural relationship between the individual candybars used in the two samples, as they are separate candybars produced at different times. You did not weigh the same candy bar before and after intervention. They are independent and not linked in any way.

        Paired situations always have the same number of data values in the two samples. Unpaired problems may or may not have the same number of data values.

    b. The 95% confidence interval for the mean difference extends from –0.0245 to 0.0345 ounces (using 2.024 from the t table, 0.01459 as the small-sample standard error, and 0.005=1.663–1.658 as the average difference).

    c. No, it did not produce a significant change in weight ($p > 0.05$). The reference value (0) is in the confidence interval. The t statistic (0.005/0.01459 = 0.34) is less than the t table value (2.024).

45. a. There is a significant difference in the product ratings of shy and outgoing consumers, using a two-sample unpaired t test. The 95% confidence interval for the mean difference in ratings (shy minus outgoing) extends from 0.085 to 0.755 (using 1.960 from the t table and 0.171110 as the large-sample standard error) and does not include the reference value 0. The t statistic is 2.45.

    b. Shy consumers give significantly higher ratings than do outgoing customers ($p < 0.05$). This is the one-sided conclusion to a two-sided test. Note that the test result is not significant at the 1% level since the t statistic (2.45) is less in absolute value than the t table value (2.576).

47. a. The difference is not significant. The 95% confidence interval for the mean difference (shy minus outgoing) extends from –0.20 to 0.56 (using 1.960 from

the *t* table and 0.19185 as the large-sample standard error) and does not include the reference value 0. The *t* statistic is 0.94.

b. The differences between shy and outgoing consumers are not significant ($p > 0.05$).

Chapter 11: Correlation and Regression

Measuring and Predicting Relationships

Odd Problem Solutions

1. a.

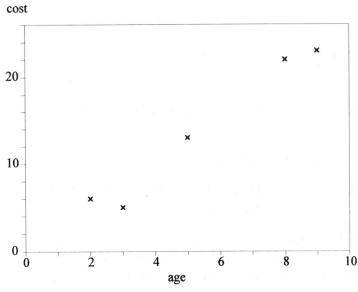

The scatterplot shows a linear structure with data values distributed about a straight line, with some randomness.

   b.   The correlation, r, between age and maintenance cost is 0.985. This correlation is very close to 1 indicating a strong positive relationship. It agrees with the scatterplot which showed the maintenance cost increasing along a straight line, with increasing age.

   c.   Predicted Cost $= -1.0645 + 2.7527$ Age

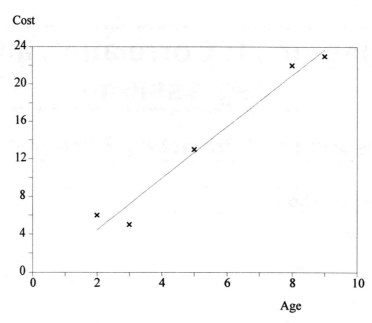

d. Predicted Cost = –1.06451+(2.752688)(7) = 18.204, in thousands of dollars, hence $18,204.

e. S_e = 1.7248, in thousands of dollars, or $1,725.

f. R^2 = 96.9% of the variation in maintenance cost can be attributed to the fact that some presses are older than others.

g. Yes, age does explain a significant amount of the variation in maintenance cost. This may be verified by testing whether the slope is significantly different from 0. The confidence interval for the slope, from 1.8527 to 3.6526, does not include 0; therefore the slope is significantly different from 0. Alternatively, note that the t statistic, $t = b/S_b = 2.7527/0.2828 = 9.73$, exceeds the t table value (3.182) for 5–2 = 3 degrees of freedom and may also be used to decide significance.

h. The extra annual cost is significantly different from $20,000. From part g, we know the we are 95% sure that the long-term yearly cost for annual maintenance per machine is somewhere between $1,853 and $3,653 per year. Since the reference value, $20,000, is not in the confidence interval, you conclude that the annual maintenance cost per year per printing press is significantly different from $20,000. In fact, it is significantly less than your conservative associate's estimate of $20,000. The t statistic is (2.752688–20)/0.282790 = –61.0.

Since the value for the t statistic is larger than the critical value (12.294 with 3 degrees of freedom) at the 0.001 level, you reject the null hypothesis and accept the research hypothesis that the population maintenance cost is different from the reference value, and claim that the finding is very highly significant ($p <$ 0.001).

3. a.

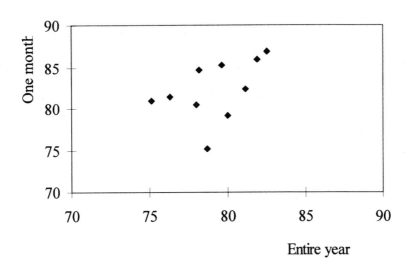

There may be a weak to moderate linear relationship here, with better entire-year performance implying better one-month performance, but there is also considerable randomness suggesting possibly no relationship.

b. The correlation is $r = 0.465$, suggesting a moderate (not a strong) positive relationship between these two performance measures.

c. $R^2 = 0.216$, indicating that 21.6% of the variability in one-month performance can be explained by entire-year performance.

d. (Predicted one-month performance) = 26.3746+0.7063(one-year performance)

e. (Predicted Alaska Airlines one month) = 26.3746+(0.7063)(76.3) = 80.3

This says that we would have expected Alaska Airlines to have performance of 80.3 for the month, based on the entire year's performance.

(Residual value Alaska Airlines) = Actual Y – Predicted Y = 81.4–80.3 = 1.1.

This says that Alaska's one-month performance was 1.1 more than the 80.3 predicted based on the entire year.

f. The standard error of estimate, $S_e = 3.375$, indicates the typical size of prediction errors.

g. $S_b = 0.4751$.

h. The 95% confidence interval extends from -0.39 to 1.80 (using 2.306 from the t table with 10–2=8 degrees of freedom).

i. The relationship is not significant because the reference value $\beta_0 = 0$ is in the confidence interval. Alternatively, the t statistic (1.49) is smaller in absolute value than the t table value (2.306). This tells you that there is no evidence here of a pattern of consistency in on-time performance. A data set like this could reasonably have arisen from a situation with no true relationship.

5.   a.   Predicted Millions of Dollars = –1,659.86+293.65(Number of Deals).

       b.   One additional deal adds the slope coefficient to the number of dollars. Thus a single additional deal adds an estimated $293.65 (millions) to the total dollar amount.

       c.

Dollar Amounts (Billions)

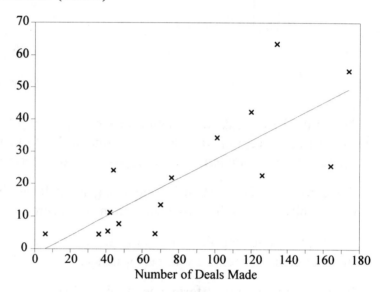

Number of Deals Made

       d.   The expected dollar amount for Goldman Sachs, with 134 deals:

$$= -1,659.86+(293.65)(134) = \$37,689 \text{ million.}$$

This is the dollar amount (37,689 million) we would predict for an investment banker with 134 deals.

The residual value is:

$$= Y-Y_0 = 63,465-37,689 = \$25,776 \text{ million.}$$

This shows that Goldman Sachs handled 25,776 (million) more than we would have expected for an investment banker handling 134 deals.

       e. $S_b = 63.24380$, measuring how far the estimated slope b (the regression coefficient computed from the sample) differs from the (idealized) population slope, β, due to the randomness of sampling.

       f.   The 95% confidence interval extends from (millions) $157.04 to $430.26 (using 2.160 from the t table).

You are 95% sure that the expected marginal value of an additional deal is between $157.04 and $430.26 (millions).

g. There is a significant relationship. This may be seen from the confidence interval (from the previous part) that does not include 0, or from the t statistic (293.65/63.2438 = 4.64) that exceeds the t table value (2.160).

h. The 95% confidence interval extends from \$890 to \$54,520 (millions, using 2.160 from the t table and \$12,414.35 million as the standard error of a new observation given X_0).

7. a.

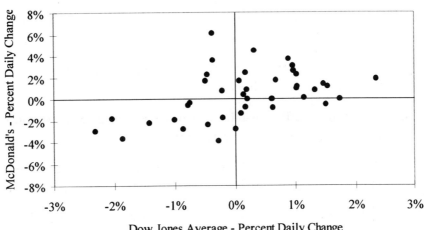

b. This is a positive linear relationship. There is a cloud of data values scattered around a line extending from lower left to upper right.

c. $r = 0.4610$. The correlation confirms the impression given by the scatterplot: a moderate positive relationship formed by a cloud of data points.

d. Coefficient of determination = $R^2 = 0.21249$. The coefficient of determination tells you how much of the variability of Y, (the daily percentage change in McDonald's stock price) is explained by the daily percentage change in the value of the X, (the daily percentage change in the value of the DJI). Market movements explain 21.2% of the changes in McDonald's stock, with 78.8% left unexplained. Apparently 21.2% of the risk of McDonald's is nondiversifiable.

e. The diversifiable risk, $1-R^2 = 78.8\%$. This proportion of the risk of McDonald's stock can be diversified away.

f. The least-squares regression equation is

McDonald's = 0.0008924+0.2115 Dow Jones.

Note that the intercept would be 0.08924 (with slope unchanged) if data were entered, e.g., as 1.33 instead of 0.0133 for 1.33%.

The slope coefficient (McDonald's beta) is $b = 0.2115$.

g. We are 95% sure that the population slope coefficient (McDonald's "true" beta) is between 0.085 and 0.338 using 1.960 from the t table. (A more exact computer confidence interval is from 0.081 to 0.342)

h. Yes, there is significant association between percent changes of McDonald's and the Dow Jones Index. The confidence interval for the slope (above) does not include 0. Alternatively, note that the t statistic is $0.2115/0.06443 = 3.28$.

i. Yes, McDonald's beta is significantly different from 1. The confidence interval for the population slope (from 0.085 to 0.338) does not include the reference value 1. Alternatively, note that the t statistic is $(0.2115-1)/.06443 = -12.24$.

You may conclude that the beta for McDonald's is significantly different from the beta of a highly diversified portfolio.

9. a. The slope coefficient tells you that each additional person brings in $0.237 (or 23.7 cents) of additional sales, on average.

b. $R^2 = 0.7967$, so 79.7% of the variation in sales is attributable to territory size. This leaves $100\%-79.7\% = 20.3\%$ of sales variation as due to other factors.

c. Yes, territory size has a significant impact on sales because the confidence interval for the regression coefficient does not include 0. The confidence interval is from 0.1298 to 0.3437 (using 2.365 from the t table and $S_b = 0.045202$). Alternatively, compare the t statistic $0.23675/0.045202 = 5.24$ to the t table value 2.365 for $9-2=7$ degrees of freedom.

d. The slope is highly significantly different from 0 ($p < 0.01$). This is based on the t statistic (5.24) compared to the t table critical values for 5%, 1%, and 0.1% which are 2.365, 3.499, and 5.408.

11. a. 1.960. b. 3.012. c. 2.069. d. 3.291.

13. a. $r = 0.5246$, indicating moderate positive association.

b. Predicted Capacity = 3,296.124+0.18115(Existing Units).

c. Residual for Highline is –1,118.

d. The 95% confidence interval extends from –0.1125 to 0.4748.

e. No, the relationship is not significant because 0 is in the confidence interval from part d. The t statistic is 1.51.

15. a. $r = 0.5028$.

b. (Predicted Price on 2/26/91) = –21.6207+0.9766(Price on 11/30/90).

c. Residual for Lynnwood = –1.9777.

d. The 95% confidence interval extends from –2.1086 to 4.0619.

e.   No. The slope coefficient is not significantly different from zero because 0 is in the confidence interval from part d. The t statistic is 1.01.

17. a. $r = 0.9987$, indicating a very strong positive association. Larger lists are associated with higher sales.

b.   Predicted Sales = 1,393.83+24.1121 (List Size), both in thousands.

c.   Predicted Sales = 1,514 (thousands).

d. $R^2 = 0.9973$, so 99.73% of the variation is explained.

e.   Yes. The relationship is significant because 0 is not in the confidence interval for b (from 22.87 to 25.36). The t statistic, 47.45, indicates very high significance.

19. a.   Predicted Production = 232.61+40.54 Workers.

b. $b = 40.54$.

c.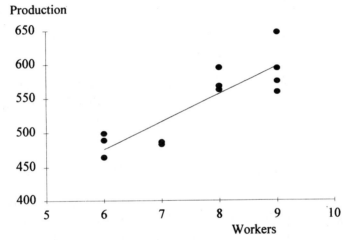

d.   Expected Production = 516.39, indicating that we expect production to be 516.39, on average, when 7 workers are assigned. Residual = –33.39, indicating that on this day (corresponding to the first pair in the data set) the actual production was 33.39 lower than expected.

e. $S_b = 7.3220$, indicating the uncertainty in the estimated slope b.

f.   The 95% confidence interval extends from 24.2 to 56.9.

g.   Yes there is a significant relationship. The confidence interval in part f does not include 0. The t statistic is 5.54.

21. Predicted value is 510.6. (The correlation value is not needed).

23. $r = 0.73$.

25. You would expect $73,952, computed as the predicted value from the least squares equation which has $a = 43,095$ and $b = 308,571$ (alternatively, divide b by 100 if you express 10% as 10 instead of 0.1; the predicted value will still be the same).

27. Unequal variability (with increasing relationship).

29. a.
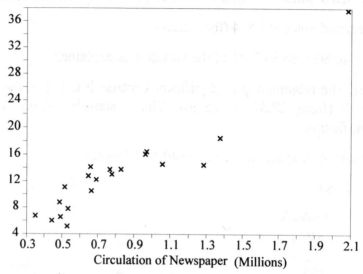

   b. $r = 0.930$. The correlation coefficient is quite close to one, indicating a very strong positive relationship. This is very reasonable from a business standpoint, since newspapers with larger circulations should charge correspondingly higher rates for ads placed only once because a larger audience is reached.

   c. Predicted Open Line Rate $= 0.28218 + 0.00001581$ Circulation.

   d. The relationship is significant. In fact, it is very highly significant ($p < 0.001$). The estimated slope is $b = 0.00001581$ with standard error $S_b = 0.000001469$ and t statistic 10.76 that exceeds the t table value (2.101) with $n-2 = 18$ degrees of freedom. Alternatively, the 99.9% confidence interval (from 0.0000100 to 0.0000216) does not include 0.

   e. Predicted value $= 0.28218 + (0.00001581)(970,051) = 15.62$.

   Residual value $=$ actual$-$predicted $= 16.47 - 15.62 = 0.85$.

   The predicted value says that, for a newspaper with circulation 970,051, we expect an open line rate of 15.62, on average. The residual value says that The New York Times has an open line rate that exceeds this expected value by 0.85. In particular, the open line rate for The New York Times is higher than you would expect for a newspaper with this circulation size.

31. a.

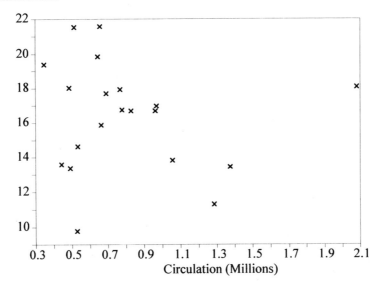

b.   Correlation coefficient = −0.125. The relationship between circulation and milline rate is very weak, since the correlation is close to 0. This confirms what was observed in the scatterplot, namely, that the data set forms a cloud of points with essentially no overall tilt.

c.   Only $R^2 = 1.56\%$ of the variation in milline rate is explained by circulation.

d.   The relationship is not significant ($p > 0.05$). The estimated slope is $b = -0.0000009703$ with standard error $S_b = 0.000001815$ and t statistic −0.53 that does not exceed the t table value (2.101) with $n–2 = 18$ degrees of freedom (in absolute value, i.e., 0.53 is less than 2.101). Alternatively, the 95% confidence interval (from −0.00000478 to 0.00000284) includes 0.

e.   When advertising rates are expressed in a "per circulation" basis (as the milline rate does) there is no relationship between rates and circulation. We have not found any tendency for larger newspapers to charge more on a per person basis than smaller newspapers. (The significant relationship found in the previous problem between open line rate and circulation showed that larger newspapers charge more per ad than smaller ones do).

Chapter 12: Multiple Regression

Predicting One Factor from Several Others

Odd Problem Solutions

1. Y = Number of leads, X_1 = Cost, X_2 = Size. Appropriate test: F test.

3. Y = Revenues, X_1 = Total Assets, X_2 = Lumbermill Capacity. Appropriate statistic: predicted value of Y (from prediction equation) using your values for the X variables.

5. a. Price = 8,344.005 + 0.026260 Area − 4.26699 Year.

   b. The value of each additional square centimeter is $26.26. All else being equal (i.e., for a given year) for an increase in area of 1 square centimeter, the price of the painting would rise by ($1,000)(0.026260) = 26.26 on average.

   c. Holding area constant, the regression coefficient for year reveals that as the years increased the price a painting could command decreased by $4,266.99 a year on average. The earlier paintings are more valuable than the later ones.

   d. Price = 8,344.005+(0.026260)(4,000)−(4.26699)(1954).

      = $111.348 (Thousands) = $111,348.

   e. The prediction errors are about $153,111. The standard error of estimate, S = 153.111, indicates the typical size of prediction errors in this data set, in thousands of dollars (because Y is in these thousands).

   f. R^2 = 28.2% of the variation in price of Picasso paintings can be attributed to the size of the painting and the year in which it was painted.

   g. Yes, the regression is significant.

      The F test done using R^2 is significant (R^2 = 0.282 with n = 23 cases and k = 2 X-variables, exceeds the table value of 0.259). This indicates that the variables, area and year taken together, explain a significant fraction of the variation in price from one painting to another.

      The traditional F test reports significance, F = 3.93203 with 2 and 20 degrees of freedom. (The p-value is 0.036).

   h. Yes, area does have a significant impact on price following adjustment for year. Larger paintings are worth significantly more than smaller ones from the same year.

The confidence interval extends from 0.000896 to 0.051623; it does not include the reference value of zero, so we accept the research hypothesis. Also, the t statistic (2.16) is larger than the critical t value (2.086) for 20 degrees of freedom. (The p-value is 0.043).

   i.   Yes, year has a significant impact on price, adjusting for area. The impact of year on price is of a decrease of price, so that newer paintings are worth significantly less than older ones of the same size.

        The confidence interval extends from –8.0048 to –0.5291 and does not include the reference value of zero. Also, the t statistic of –2.38 is larger in absolute value than the critical t table value of 2.086. (The p-value is 0.027).

7. a.   More.

    b.   The regression coefficient for Weight, 73.17, indicates the (positive) additional average cost associated with an increase in weight of one unit. The measurement units are dollars per unit of weight. Yes it is significant ($t = 4.76$, $p < 0.0005$).

    c.   No. We had expected that, for tents of a given area, the lighter tents would cost more (and heavier tents less). Instead we find that heavier tents cost more on average than lighter ones with the same area.

         There may be other factors involved than just area and weight. If heavier tents are heavier because they have more useful features, then we would expect to see higher cost for heavier tents. Instead of campers paying extra for weight (which doesn't make a lot of sense) they might be paying for extra features.

    d.   Less.

    e.   The regression coefficient for Area, –7.517, indicates the (negative) additional average cost associated with an increase in area of one unit. The measurement units are dollars per unit of area. Yes it is significant ($t = -2.95$, $p = 0.006$).

    f.   No. We had expected larger tents to cost more, all else equal. Instead, we find that larger tents cost less on average than smaller ones that weigh the same.

         There may be other factors involved than just area and weight. In order to keep weight constant, it may be necessary to decrease area in order to add useful features to the tent. Instead of campers paying extra for a smaller tent (which doesn't make a lot of sense) they might be paying for extra features.

9. Exercise for the student. Stock market performance in Europe and the Pacific Rim explains only $R^2 = 9.0\%$ of the variation in U.S. stock market performance. The F test is not significant ($F = 0.55$ with 2 and 11 degrees of freedom; the p-value is 0.594). There is no significant connection between these international markets and U.S. performance, according to this particular data set.

11. a.   The standard error of estimate, 149.356 representing $149,356, is the approximate size of the prediction errors. This answer, S_e, is in thousands because Y is in thousands.

b.   Predicted Pay $= 583.3609 + 0.004369$ Sales $+ 30.38801$ ROE.

$= 583.3609+(0.004369)(77,721)+(30.38801)(15.0).$

$= 1,379$ (thousands) $= \$1,379,000$

Residual $= 1,207 - 1,379 = -172$ (thousands) $= -\$172,000.$

This executive is paid $172,000 less than we would expect for a firm with this level of sales and ROE.

c.   Yes, the t test for ROE is significant. The confidence interval does not include zero, the test result is given, and the t statistic (3.64) exceeds the t table value (2.306) for $n–k–1 = 11–2–1 = 8$ degrees of freedom. Furthermore, the F test is also significant (using either the F or the R^2 table) so we are permitted to examine the t statistics.

d.   For a fixed level of sales, every 1% (one percentage point) increase in ROE is associated with an additional $30,388 (30.38801 in thousands) of compensation for top executives.

e.   This is because the data set is small, with only $n = 11$ cases. With $n–k–1 = 11–2–1 = 8$ degrees of freedom, the t table value is 2.306 (larger than the 1.960 or 2 we usually think of for larger data sets). Since the t statistic does not exceed the t table value (in absolute value) it is not significant.

13. a. $R^2 = 79.7\%$ of the variation in cost is explained by the information available.

b.   To within about one standard error of estimate, $3,860.

c.   Predicted cost is $57,396 (you will find one dollar less if you use the lower precision regression coefficients in the regression equation instead of the higher precision numbers in the table that follows after).

d.   Yes the F test is significant. This tells you that information about labor and materials, taken together, explains a significant amount of the variation in final cost from one contract to another.

$R^2 = 0.797$ is larger than the tabled value (0.238 for $n = 25$ and $k = 2$). $F = 43.17$ with 2 and 22 degrees of freedom. The p-value 0.000 ($p < 0.0005$) is listed in the printout next to F.

e.   Yes, materials does have a significant impact on cost. The t statistic is 5.97, with $p < 0.0005$.

15. a.   Of course you can explain profits using revenues and costs because of the basic relationship

   Profits = Revenues–Costs.

   Since this relationship holds exactly, multiple regression will find it and therefore 100% of the variation in profits will be "explained".

   b.   Regression coefficients: Revenues 1, Costs –1.

17. We expect a reduction of $(0.62)(7.290)–(0.38)(7.290) = 1.75$ percentage points in the defect rate, on average, all else equal. This assumes that, when switching suppliers, you also manage to hold all else equal. If this decision also interacts with other parts of the process, then the expected reduction may be different.

19. Multicollinearity.

21. a.   Predicted Profit = 22,085.37–1,112.87 Price.

   b.   The regression coefficient is not significant ($t = –1.53$). Since there is just one X variable, we may use the t test for its regression coefficient (the F test, either based on $R^2 = 28.0\%$ or on $F = 2.337$, gives the same answer). The 95% confidence interval extends from –2,894.16 to 668.42, based on the coefficient (–1,112.87), its standard error (727.9496), and the t table value (2.447) with $n–k–1 = 8–1–1 = 6$ degrees of freedom. Alternatively, consider the t statistic (–1.53) which does not exceed the t table value (2.447) in absolute value.

   At first glance, this result does not seem reasonable because in business we expect to find a relationship between price and profit. In fact, from just scanning the data you can see that there is a clear relationship between price and profit. This relationship does not, however, appear linear and this may be why ordinary linear regression did not find it.

   c.   The profit can be predicted to within approximately $4,718, the standard error of estimate.

d.   Residuals (thousands)

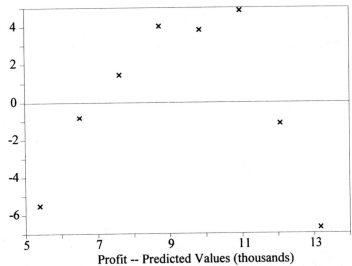

Profit -- Predicted Values (thousands)

There is substantial nonlinear structure in this diagnostic plot. It is not just a random scatter; the graph shows a curved inverted U-shaped relationship.

e.

Profit	Price	Price^2
6,486	8	64
10,928	9	81
15,805	10	100
13,679	11	121
12,758	12	144
9,050	13	169
5,702	14	196
−109	15	225

Predicted Profit $= -87,891.3 + 18,804.17$ Price $- 865.958$ Price^2.

f. The profit can be predicted to within approximately $1,229, the standard error of estimate. Note that this is much smaller than the $4,718 found predicting from price alone.

g. Price and squared price, taken together, do explain a significant proportion of the variation in profit. The R^2 value (0.959) exceeds the table value (0.698) for $n = 8$ observations and $k = 2$ variables. The F statistic is 58.9 with 2 and 5 degrees of freedom. (The p-value is 0.000335).

Note that 95.9% of the variation in profit can be explained by price and price squared. Only 28% of the profit was explained by use of price alone.

h. The optimal price is at $-b_1/(2b_2) = -18,804.17/[2\,(-865.958)] = \$10.86$. This is fairly close to the price, $10, that yielded the highest profit ($15,805) in the original data table.

It is interesting to note that the estimated optimal price, $10.86, is closer to $11 than to $10, even though $10 gave the highest profit in the test markets. These answers are slightly different because the estimate based on regression ($10.86) is using more information from the whole data set than just looking at the highest profit. Thus the randomness of a single observation cannot overly influence the results.

23 a.   Percent Male is the variable least helpful in explaining page costs. Its standardized regression coefficient (–0.014) is much smaller in absolute value than the others. The other standardized regression coefficients are 0.863 for Circulation and 0.227 for Median Income.

    b.   Predicted Page Costs = –8,251.72 + 5.286788 Circulation + 1.184900 Income

         $S_e = 12985.55$. $R^2 = 0.694075$. $F = 51.04748$ with 2 and 45 degrees of freedom.

         Standard errors of coefficients: Constant 11,850.22, Circulation 0.523270, and Income 0.460240.

    c.

Statistic	With Percent Male	Without Percent Male
F test Value	33.30	51.05
F test degrees of freedom	3 and 44	2 and 45
F test Significant?	Yes	Yes
R^2	0.694	0.694
Circulation: coefficient	5.2815	5.2868
Circulation: t statistic	9.958	10.103
Median income: coefficient	1.2226	1.1849
Median income: t statistic	2.283	2.575

Without the omitted third variable the F test is still significant, and the R^2 value, indicating the percent of variation in page costs explained by the variables, is essentially unchanged. The regression coefficient for circulation is very little changed. There is a slight change in the regression coefficient for median income. Both t statistics have changed slightly. In all, the removal of the variable which had contributed so little to the variation originally (its t statistic was very small, –0.142) produced little change in the regression analysis when it was removed.

Chapter 13: Report Writing

Communicating the Results of a Multiple Regression

Odd Problem Solutions

1. a. Purpose: to provide background information on the size of shipping facilities at other firms to help with expansion strategy. Audience: those executives who will be suggesting plans and making decisions about this expansion.

    b. Purpose: to provide information on this new product and to help with marketing efforts. Audience: readers of the magazine who will be deciding which system to purchase or recommend to others.

    c. Purpose: to provide information concerning breakdowns and their causes so that some of these problems can be fixed. Audience: those who can take action to fix these problems.

    d. Purpose: to demonstrate that your firm is not too vulnerable to financial trouble in a recession. Audience: Bankers who will be deciding your firm's credit limit.

3. Exercise for the student. They should provide orientation, information, and results, but not details.

5. a. J.A. White, "How a Money Manager Can Pull a Rabbit Out of a Hat," The Wall Street Journal, March 16, 1989, p. C1.

    b. Professor Lawrence D. Schall, University of Washington, personal communication, [insert date here].

    c. From H. Gitlow, S. Gitlow, and A. Oppenheim, Tools and Methods for the Improvement of Quality (Homewood, Ill.: Richard D. Irwin, 1989), Chapter 8.

    d. From The Conference Board, "Business Cycle Indicators, Latest Releases," http://www.tcb-indicators.org/, January 26, 1999 (accessed February 4, 1999) .

Chapter 14: Time Series

Understanding Changes over Time

Odd Problem Solutions

1. a. Strong seasonal component because of the December holiday season.

    b. Strong seasonal component due to holiday vacations in December, winter months, and also (perhaps) summer vacations.

    c. No strong seasonal components because such predictable "profit opportunities" cannot exist in efficient markets.

3. a. $13.4\% = (43,182-38,091)/38,091$.

    b. $6.6\% = (0.986-0.925) / 0.925$.

    c. January: 41,179. February: 43,795, seasonally adjusted by dividing by seasonal index.

    d. $6.4\% = (43,795-41,179)/41,179$.

5. a.

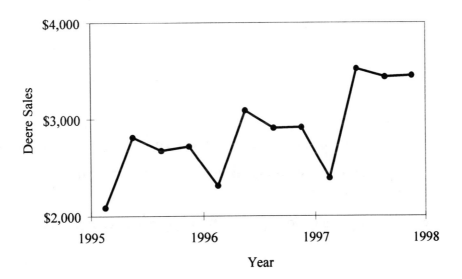

    There is an overall increasing trend over time with seasonal variation.

    b. The moving average is not available for the first two quarters of 1995. The first value is for third quarter 1995: $(2,088/2+2,812+2,673+2,718+2,318/2)/4 = \$2,602$. This and the other moving average values are shown below:

Year	Sales (millions)	Moving Average
1995	2,088	(unavailable)
1995	2,812	(unavailable)
1995	2,673	2,602
1995	2,718	2,665
1996	2,318	2,729
1996	3,089	2,782
1996	2,905	2,817
1996	2,917	2,881
1997	2,396	3,000
1997	3,521	3,132
1997	3,430	(unavailable)
1997	3,444	(unavailable)

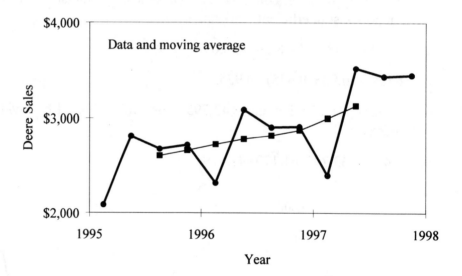

c. The seasonal indices for quarters 1 through 4 are: 0.824, 1.117, 1.029, and 1.016. Yes, these seem reasonable: quarter 1 is always lower than its neighbors.

d. Quarter 1 is the worst. Sales are $1-0.824 = 17.6\%$ lower as compared to a typical quarter.

e. Dividing each sales figure by the appropriate seasonal index:

Year	Sales (millions)	Seasonally adjusted
1995	2,088	2,534
1995	2,812	2,517
1995	2,673	2,597
1995	2,718	2,675
1996	2,318	2,813
1996	3,089	2,765
1996	2,905	2,822
1996	2,917	2,870
1997	2,396	2,908
1997	3,521	3,152
1997	3,430	3,332
1997	3,444	3,389

f. On a seasonally adjusted basis, sales also went up from third to fourth quarter of 1995 (from 2,597 to 2,675).

g. On a seasonally adjusted basis, sales rose from the second to the third quarter of 1997 (from 3,152 to 3,332).

h. The regression equation using the time period 1, 2, 3, ... for X and the seasonally adjusted series for Y is:

Predicted Adjusted Sales = 2,363 + 76.998 (Time Period).

i. Predicted Sales = 4,058, found by substituting 22 for Time Period.

j. The forecast is 3,534. The seasonally adjusted forecast is found from the regression equation using Time Period = 25 to find Predicted Adjusted Sales = 4,289. Seasonalizing (multiplying by the first quarter seasonal index) we find the forecast (4,289)(0.824) = 3,534.

7. a.

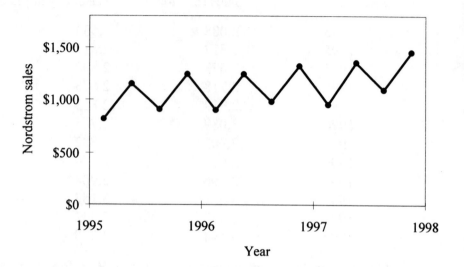

There are strong seasonal components here, with quarters 1 and 3 consistently low, and quarters 2 and 4 consistently high. There is little cyclic variation. Irregular behavior is evident in that the seasonal pattern does not exactly repeat each year.

b. Quarters 2 and 4 are generally Nordstrom's best.

c. Yes.

d.

Year	Nordstrom, Inc. Sales (millions)	Moving average
1995	816	
1995	1,149	
1995	907	1,040
1995	1,242	1,063
1996	906	1,084
1996	1,241	1,103
1996	984	1,119
1996	1,321	1,139
1997	954	1,166
1997	1,353	1,196
1997	1,090	
1997	1,455	

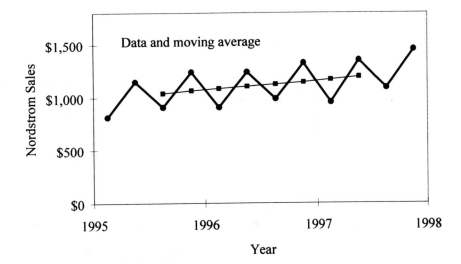

e. There is little, if any, cyclic variation here, as is seen from the moving average which increases steadily without wandering up and down.

f. The seasonal indices for quarters 1 through 4 are: 0.827, 1.128, 0.876, and 1.164. Yes, these seem reasonable: quarters 1 and 3 are low, while quarters 2 and 4 are high in general.

g.

Year	Nordstrom, Inc. Sales (millions)	Seasonally adjusted
1995	816	987
1995	1,149	1,019
1995	907	1,036
1995	1,242	1,067
1996	906	1,095
1996	1,241	1,100
1996	984	1,123
1996	1,321	1,135
1997	954	1,154
1997	1,353	1,199
1997	1,090	1,245
1997	1,455	1,250

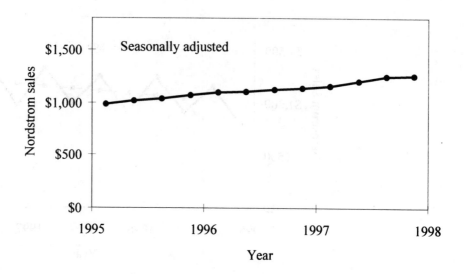

h.   Yes, there is an overall upward linear trend. It might be appropriate to use a regression line to forecast this series if we expect the steady growth to continue in the future.

9. a.   5,423+(17)(408) = 12,359.

    b.   5,423+(18)(408) = 12,767.

    c.   Because these are seasonally adjusted: the expected seasonal downturn has been removed, and we are seeing the overall increasing trend.

    d.   (12,359)(1.45) = 17,920.6.

    e.   (12,767)(0.55) = 7,021.9.

    f.   408.

    g.   Yearly total forecast for 2003:

         22,653.4+ 8,817.1+11,836.1+21,227.2 = 64,533.8.

      Yearly total forecast for 2004:

         25,019.8+ 9,714.7+13,011.1+23,283.5 = 71,029.1.

      The first such year is 2004.

11. Trend-seasonal analysis.

13. a.   This should be nonstationary because stock prices tend to follow a random walk.

     b.   This may be stationary because interest rates do not wander off towards higher and higher (or lower and lower) values.

c. Stationary because the process is in control and the thickness will not wander off too far in either direction.

d. Nonstationary because prices tend to increase over time due to inflation.

15. a. This is an autoregressive moving-average (ARMA) process.

b. They are all significant because all t statistics exceed 1.960 in absolute value.

c. Yes, this would be surprising because 15 is below the lower forecast limit.

d. No, this would not be surprising because 120 is within the forecast limits.

e. No, we do not expect the index to stop changing in the future. However, our ability to forecast these changes is limited, especially for longer time horizons. We use the *expected value* of the random future behavior of the estimated model as the forecast; being an average the forecast shows less variability than the series itself.

17. a. The autoregressive (AR) component is included.

b. No, the AR term is not significant ($t = 0.04$ is less than 1.960 in absolute value).

c. Yes, the constant term is significant ($t = -4.05$) and indicates that the work week has been declining at a rate of 0.16 hours or 9.6 minutes per year, since $-9.6 = (-0.15943)(60)$. Because the data have been differenced (so that an Integrated Moving Average process has been fitted), the constant term -0.15943 represents the estimated average yearly long-term decline in the work week, not the length of the work week.

d. No, this would not be surprising because 33.5 is within the forecast limits.

e. Yes, this would be surprising because 37.5 hours is well above the upper forecast limit.

Chapter 15: ANOVA

Testing for Differences among Many Samples, and Much More

Odd Problem Solutions

1. a. Ad #2 appears to have the highest effectiveness (68.1). Ad #3 appears to have the lowest effectiveness (53.5).

    b. The total sample size is $n = 303$. The grand average is $\bar{X} = 61.4073$. The number of samples is $k = 3$.

    c. The between-sample variability is 5,617.30 with $k-1 = 2$ degrees of freedom.

    d. The within-sample variability is 91.006 with $n-k = 300$ degrees of freedom.

3. a. The critical value is 6.908 (for 2 and infinity degrees of freedom as an approximation) at the 0.1% level. Reject the null hypothesis. The F test is very highly significant because the F statistic is larger than this critical value. The difference between the three ads is very highly significant. ($p < 0.001$).

    b. This test has told you that there is a very highly significant difference in consumer response to the three ads which were placed in the target city. It has not told you whether all the results from the ads were different from each other, or only some were.

5. a.

	Ad 2 Minus Ad 1	Ad 1 Minus Ad 3	Ad 2 Minus Ad 3
Average Difference	4.9	9.7	14.6
Standard Error	1.35619	1.32958	1.34348

    b. All pairs of ads are highly significantly different from one another. Ad #2 has a higher average effectiveness than the other two ads. Ad #1 has the next highest effectiveness, and ad #3 shows the least effectiveness.

    The 99% confidence level for the difference between ad 1 and ad 2 extends from 1.41 to 8.39 . The t statistic is 3.61.

    The 99% confidence level for the difference between ad 1 and ad 3 extends from 6.28 to 13.12. The t statistic is 7.30.

    The 99% confidence level for the difference between ad 2 and ad 3 extends from 11.14 to 18.06. The t statistic is 10.87.

7. a. $F = 2.188$ with 2 and 27 degrees of freedom.

    b. There is more than twice as much variability (2.188 times) between samples, as exists for the data values within the individual samples. Essentially, there is twice as much variation as we would find if all the variation observed were due to the randomness of sampling from the same population.

    c. The critical value is between 3.316 and 3.493. At the 5% level for a numerator of 2 degrees of freedom and a denominator or 27 degrees of freedom, the critical value is approximately 3.316 (the critical value for 2 and 30 degrees of freedom) and is between this and 3.493 (the value for 2 and 20 degrees of freedom).

    d. Accept the null hypothesis as a reasonable possibility. The differences observed in the averages of these samples are not statistically significant and can be explained by the randomness in the situation because the F statistic is smaller than the critical value from the F table.

    e. The F test tells you that there are no significant differences among these additives. You accept the null hypothesis that they are all equally good. You have not proven that there are no differences (remember, accepting a null hypothesis is a weak conclusion); it is just that you do not have convincing evidence that there are any differences. In particular, you have no sound basis for choosing a "best" one.

9. a. The critical value is between 2.489 and 2.589. At the 10% level for 2 and 27 degrees of freedom, the critical value is approximately 2.489 (the critical value for 2 and 30 degrees of freedom) and is between this and 2.589 (the value for 2 and 20 degrees of freedom). Accept the null hypothesis.

    b. The F test shows that there is no significant difference between these three additives even at the less demanding 10% level. In using the criterion of ability to reduce waste in the manufacturing process, one would have to conclude that there is still no demonstrated advantage to using one instead of another because the F statistic, 2.1885, is smaller than the critical value from the F table at the 10% level.

11. a.

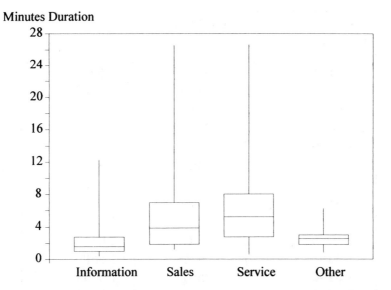

Minutes Duration

The longest telephone calls are found for sales and service; calls are generally shorter for information and for other types of calls, although there is considerable overlap. There appears to be unequal variability here: Sales and service show more variability in the time of the telephone calls (as indicated by the height of the boxes) as compared to information and other.

There is a suggestion of skewness (lack of symmetry) or outliers here: All four distributions extend further to large values than to small values (long lines from the top, small ones from the bottom of each box).

b.

	Average	Standard Deviation
Information	2.607692	3.147343
Sales	5.870588	6.620967
Service	7.193333	6.718043
Other	2.785714	1.782721

c. Service appears to have the highest average length. Information appears to have the lowest average length.

d. No, due to skewness, possible outliers, and unequal variability noted in part a.

e.

Natural Log of Information	Natural Log of Sales	Natural Log of Service	Natural Log of Other
−0.5108	1.6292	1.6487	1.8405
0.0953	0.5306	1.0647	0.1823
0.0000	1.4816	0.9555	1.1314
0.6419	3.2809	0.1823	0.9163
1.3350	2.0015	1.9459	1.0986
0.4700	0.3365	2.6532	0.9555
−0.9163	1.9459	2.1282	−0.2231
−0.5108	1.3610	−0.5108	
0.7885	1.1314	3.2847	
2.5096	0.1823	2.0412	
1.4351	0.6419	1.5686	
1.0296	2.8507	1.9741	
0.3365	2.0541	0.9933	
	1.4586	1.2238	
	1.2238	2.5878	
	0.2624		
	0.6931		

Natural Log of Duration in Minutes

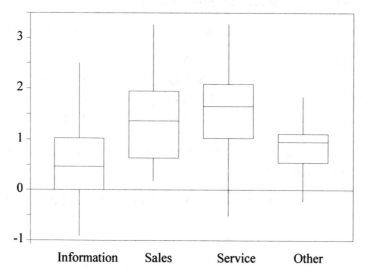

f. Yes. Examination of the box plots of the natural logs of the distributions shows symmetric distributions and fairly equal variabilities. The sizes of the boxes are quite similar. The medians are placed almost centrally in all the boxes except for "other", where it is displaced to higher values. The extreme values are not so unbalanced to one side as they were before.

13. a. $F = 3.851$ with 3 and 48 degrees of freedom.

b. The critical values is between 2.922 and 2.758. The first number, 2.922, is for 3
    and 30 degrees of freedom. The second is for 3 and 60 degrees of freedom.

c. There are significant differences in the duration of telephone calls received by
    you concerning information, sales, service, and other issues, testing at the 5%
    level. You know this because the F statistic (3.851) is larger than the critical
    value from the F table (between 2.922 and 2.758) for the 5% test level.

d. There are significant differences among telephone-call durations for these four
    groups. You now know that some groups take longer to service than others.
    Because the analysis took place on the logarithmic scale, it is not just a simple
    average difference[1] because variability was also different on the original scale.
    By taking logs, we helped the required assumptions be satisfied so that you can
    trust the test results. We do not know yet exactly which classes of phone calls
    are different from one another.

---

[1]In fact, whenever the logs are analyzed in this way, you may say that the geometric
averages are significantly different. The geometric average is defined as the nth root
of the product of the n data values. The connection is that the average of the logs is
the log of the geometric average.

15. a and b.

Y Quality Score	X_1 Indicator for Amalgamated	X_2 Indicator for Bipolar
75	1	0
72	1	0
87	1	0
77	1	0
84	1	0
82	1	0
84	1	0
81	1	0
78	1	0
97	1	0
85	1	0
81	1	0
95	1	0
81	1	0
72	1	0
89	1	0
84	1	0
73	1	0
94	0	1
87	0	1
80	0	1
86	0	1
80	0	1
67	0	1
86	0	1
82	0	1
86	0	1
82	0	1
72	0	1
77	0	1
87	0	1
68	0	1
80	0	1
76	0	1
68	0	1
86	0	1
74	0	1
86	0	1
90	0	1
90	0	0
86	0	0
92	0	0
75	0	0
79	0	0
94	0	0
95	0	0
85	0	0
86	0	0
92	0	0
92	0	0
85	0	0
87	0	0
86	0	0
92	0	0
85	0	0
93	0	0
89	0	0
83	0	0

c.   Predicted Quality $= 87.68421 - 5.62865$ Amalgamated $- 7.01754$ Bipolar. $S = 6.755$, $R^2 = 0.177$, $F = 5.897$ with 2 and 55 degrees of freedom. The F test is significant.

Variable	Coeff	95% confidence interval		Std Error	t
Constant	87.68421	84.5785	90.7899	1.54972	56.58
Amalgamated	−5.62865	−10.0814	−1.1759	2.22187	−2.53
Bipolar	−7.01754	−11.3038	−2.7312	2.13882	−3.28

d.   The F statistics are identical. Whether from multiple regression or from the one-way analysis of variance, the F statistic is 5.897. This is sensible because each is testing whether the groups are different, on average, or not. Remember that when indicator variables are used in multiple regression, a single number (the regression coefficient, representing the average difference) is added to the prediction equation when that indicator variable is "1".

e.   The regression coefficient is the same as the average difference. The regression coefficient for Amalgamated, −5.62865, is interpreted "on average, how much higher is Amalgamated than the baseline case, adjusting for the other variables." Since the baseline case is Consolidated (which was not included as an indicator variable), and since we have not adjusted for any variables other than manufacturer, the regression coefficient should be the average difference Amalgamated–Consolidated. This difference is:

Average quality difference, Amalgamated–Consolidated

$$= 82.055556 - 87.684211 = -5.628655.$$

f.   They are in complete agreement. Both are attempting to explain the differences among quality scores by grouping them by manufacturer. The multiple regression "explains" the variation in quality scores based on the indicator variables that identify the manufacturer and add an amount that depends upon which manufacturer it is. This has the effect of allowing the means to be different for each manufacturer, which is the one-way ANOVA approach.

17.   The day shift average, 80.08, is more than 7 points smaller than that of the night shift (87.48) and is about 2 points larger than the swing shift's average score. Yes, the night shift in particular is more than just a few quality points above the others. The shift-related differences are significant ($p = 0.000$, so $p < 0.0005$).

19. a.   Yes. The difference in performance between the cooperation group and the competition group is statistically significant. The performance of the cooperation group is significantly higher than the performance of the competition group.

You know the difference is significant because the p-value of 0.049682 (for the test "Competition-cooperation (A)" in the table) is smaller than 0.05, which indicates significance at the 5% level.

b.   No. Value dissensus does not have a significant impact on performance.

The p-value for value dissensus (B) is 0.792174. Any p-value greater than 0.05 indicates a nonsignificant result (tested at the conventional 5% level).

c.   The interaction of competition-cooperation and value dissensus is not significant. The p-value for this interaction, 0.469221, is greater than 0.05 and therefore the test is not significant.

This tells you that the performance measures for competition and for cooperation showed the same pattern for low value dissensus as for high value dissensus. Being careful (since this is a weak conclusion of accepting a null hypothesis) we would conclude that there is no strong evidence that the performance difference between competition and cooperation depends at all on value dissensus.

21. Yes there are significant differences among these camera angles ($p < 0.001$). The highest score was for a low angle looking up, which appears to be the best angle. (Note: while this appears to be best, we do not know whether or not it is significantly better than the second-best score).

Chapter 16: Nonparametrics

Testing with Ordinal Data or Nonnormal Distributions

Odd Problem Solutions

1. a.   Nonparametric analysis is the only method which can be used. This is ordinal data. Parametric analysis is not possible with ordinal data because it does not have numerical values.

    b.   The nonparametric method is probably preferable here. The outlier could distort a parametric analysis, but will not have undue influence on the nonparametric result.

    c.   The parametric method is preferable. Parametric methods are more efficient when data have a normal distribution.

3. a.

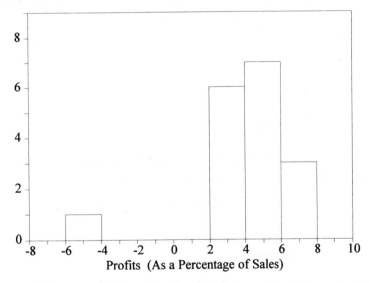

Number of Firms

Profits (As a Percentage of Sales)

The distribution is concentrated primarily between +2% and +8%, with one outlier (Sundstrand) at –5%.

    b.   The average is 3.411765 and the median is 4.0. The average and median are different. The average is smaller than the median, pulled to low values by the outlier (Sundstrand) which has a loss of 5%.

c.   Accept the research hypothesis since zero is not in the 95% confidence interval from 2.08 to 4.75 (using 2.120 from the t table). The average profit of aerospace companies is significantly different from zero. The t statistic is $3.411765/0.630469 = 5.41$, indicating that this is very highly significant.

d.   Reject the null hypothesis using the nonparametric test. The median profit is significantly different from 0. Here are the steps:

(1)   The modified sample size is 17. This is the same as the number of data values since no data value is equal to zero.

(2)   From the table, the sign test is significant at the 5% level if the number of ranked values counted is less than 5 or more than 12.

(3)   The count is that only 1 value is less than zero, this is Sundstrand with −5.

(4)   The count falls outside the limit. Therefore the median profit for this idealized population of aerospace companies is significantly different from zero.

e.   Both tests find significance in this case. The sign test is appropriate while the t test is not appropriate due to the presence of the outlier which violates the assumption of a normal distribution.

5.   Accept the null hypothesis. The difference in the median number of calls per day handled this year is not statistically significant. You are not significantly overloaded compared to last year; this could have happened due to random chance alone. Here are the details of the sign test:

(1)   24 data values are different from the reference value, which is the median number of calls per day during the past year. (Note that it is not important to know what this number is).

(2)   From the table, the sign test is significant at the 5% level if the number of ranked values counted is less than 7 or more than 17.

(3)   The count is that 9 values fall below the reference value.

(4)   The observed count, 9, is within the limits of the table. The difference is not statistically significant.

7.   a.   No. Person number 4 showed lower stress during a false answer than during a true answer.

b.   1 person (person 4) showed more stress during a true answer. 5 people (all others) showed more stress during a false answer.

c.   The modified sample size is 6 because all of the subjects changed stress level.

d. There is no significant difference between the stress level for true and false answers elicited by the methods used in this type of stress level test. Accept the null hypothesis. Here are the details:

(1) The modified sample size is 6.

(2) From the table, the sign test is significant at the 5% level if the number of ranked values counted is less than 1 or more than 5.

(3) The count of data values shows 1 data value that showed more stress during a true answer.

(4) Since the count falls at (not outside) the limits of the table for a modified sample size of 6, we accept the null hypothesis.

9. a. Median profit for building firms is 4; for aerospace firms the median is also 4. They are identical.

b.

Profit Percent	Industry
−1	Building
−2	Building
7	Building
4	Building
−59	Building
10	Building
1	Building
7	Building
7	Building
4	Building
−7	Building
−1	Building
9	Building
9	Building
4	Aerospace
4	Aerospace
2	Aerospace
7	Aerospace
4	Aerospace
6	Aerospace
4	Aerospace
3	Aerospace
2	Aerospace
6	Aerospace
2	Aerospace
3	Aerospace
4	Aerospace
5	Aerospace
−5	Aerospace
4	Aerospace
3	Aerospace

c.

Ranks with Ties Averaged	Profit Percent	Industry	Ranks (before averaging ties)
1.0	−59	Building	1
2.0	−7	Building	2
3.0	−5	Aerospace	3
4.0	−2	Building	4
5.5	−1	Building	5
5.5	−1	Building	6
7.0	1	Building	7
9.0	2	Aerospace	8
9.0	2	Aerospace	9
9.0	2	Aerospace	10
12.0	3	Aerospace	11
12.0	3	Aerospace	12
12.0	3	Aerospace	13
17.5	4	Aerospace	14
17.5	4	Aerospace	15
17.5	4	Aerospace	16
17.5	4	Aerospace	17
17.5	4	Aerospace	18
17.5	4	Building	19
17.5	4	Building	20
17.5	4	Aerospace	21
22.0	5	Aerospace	22
23.5	6	Aerospace	23
23.5	6	Aerospace	24
26.5	7	Building	25
26.5	7	Building	26
26.5	7	Building	27
26.5	7	Aerospace	28
29.5	9	Building	29
29.5	9	Building	30
31.0	10	Building	31

d.   Ranks listed by industry group:

Rank	Industry
1.0	Building
2.0	Building
4.0	Building
5.5	Building
5.5	Building
7.0	Building
17.5	Building
17.5	Building
26.5	Building
26.5	Building
26.5	Building
29.5	Building
29.5	Building
31.0	Building

Rank	Industry
3.0	Aerospace
9.0	Aerospace
9.0	Aerospace
9.0	Aerospace
12.0	Aerospace
12.0	Aerospace
12.0	Aerospace
17.5	Aerospace
17.5	Aerospace
17.5	Aerospace
17.5	Aerospace
17.5	Aerospace
17.5	Aerospace
22.0	Aerospace
23.5	Aerospace
23.5	Aerospace
26.5	Aerospace

e.   Average rank for the building group:

$$[1+2+4+(2\times5.5)+7.0+(2\times17.5)+(3\times26.5)+(2\times29.5)+31]/14$$

$$= 229.5/14 = 16.392857$$

Average rank for the aerospace group:

$$[3+(3\times9)+(3\times12)+(6\times17.5)+22+(2\times23.5)+26.5]/17$$

$$= 266.5/17 = 15.67647$$

Difference between the average ranks:

$$16.392857-15.67647 = 0.716387$$

f.   Standard error for the difference in the ranks:

$$(14+17)\sqrt{\frac{14+17+1}{12\times14\times17}} = 3.281388.$$

g.   Test Statistic = 0.716387 / 3.281388 = 0.218.

h.   The test statistic of 0.218 is less than the critical value of 1.960. This indicates that there is no significant difference between the profits made by the building industry and the aerospace industry. You accept the null hypothesis. The observed differences between the profits made by the building industry and the aerospace industry are not statistically significant. These observable differences can be explained by the randomness of sampling. This conclusion is very reasonable, considering the fact that the medians are identical.

11. a.   Median days to failure:

            Your product: 3.35
            Your competitor's product: 2.00
            Difference: 1.35, with your products lasting longer.

   b.   The test statistic is 2.00, using the nonparametric test for two unpaired samples:

Rank	Days	Producer		Rank	Days	Producer
1	0.2	Competitor		15	2.5	Competitor
2.5	0.5	Competitor		16	2.6	Competitor
2.5	0.5	Competitor		17	2.8	Competitor
4	1.0	You		18	2.9	You
6	1.2	Competitor		19	3.1	You
6	1.2	Competitor		20	3.6	You
6	1.2	You		21	4.9	You
8	1.7	Competitor		22	5.3	You
9	1.8	You		23	6.6	Competitor
10	1.9	Competitor		24	7.2	Competitor
11	2.0	Competitor		25	8.6	You
12	2.1	You		26	8.9	You
13	2.2	Competitor		27	10.3	You
14	2.3	Competitor				

Separating by producer, we have

Rank	Producer	Rank	Producer
4	You	1	Competitor
6	You	2.5	Competitor
9	You	2.5	Competitor
12	You	6	Competitor
18	You	6	Competitor
19	You	8	Competitor
20	You	10	Competitor
21	You	11	Competitor
22	You	13	Competitor
25	You	14	Competitor
26	You	15	Competitor
27	You	16	Competitor
		17	Competitor
		23	Competitor
		24	Competitor

The average rank for your product is 17.41667, the average rank for your competitor's product is 11.26667, the difference in average ranks is 6.15, the standard error is 3.074085, and the test statistic is the ratio (17.41667–11.26667)/3.074085 = 2.0006.

c. Accept the research hypothesis. The test statistic of 2.00 is larger than the critical value of 1.960, indicating that there is a statistically significant difference between the reliability of your product and your competitor's product. Your product is significantly more reliable.

d. Exercise for the student. Something along the lines of "studies show that our products are significantly more reliable than others on the market[1] ..."

13. The differences are not significant. This is a paired situation.

The cabernet was rated higher by 4 experts and there are no ties. According to the table of ranks for the sign test, in order to find significance with modified sample size 10 we would need to find either less than 2 or more than 8 experts preferring a particular vintage.

15. a. This is a paired situation.

---

[1]Our median days to failure was found to be 3.35, but was only 2.00 for the competitor. This difference was shown to be statistically significant ($p < 0.05$) using a nonparametric test.

b. The prices are significantly higher in the United States. All 10 drugs cost more in the U.S. The modified sample size is 10 and the limits for significance at the 5% level are "less than 2 or more than 8".

Chapter 17: Chi-Squared Analysis

Testing for Patterns in Qualitative Data

Odd Problem Solutions

1. a. No, not necessarily. The assumptions to be met for performing a chi-squared test are: (1) the data set should be a random sample from the population of interest and (2) at least five counts are expected in each category. The second condition is met; the expected count is 8.61. If the data set is a random sample from the population of interest there would be no problems with going ahead with the chi-squared test.

    b. Yes, there is a problem here. There are only 3.29 expected counts where the minimum required number is 5.

3. a.

Type	Percent of total, first day of the month	Percent of total, this month last year
Reservation	33.1%	33.2%
Information	33.8%	38.1%
Service request	17.5%	12.5%
Cancellation	11.3%	9.7%
Other	4.4%	6.5%
TOTAL	100.0%	100.0%

Compared to last years percentages, the percentage reservations is essentially unchanged from last year. There is a somewhat larger percentage of service requests and cancellations than was found last year. Phone calls for information and other have decreased in this time period.

b.

Type	Percent of total, this month last year	Expected number of calls, first day of the month
Reservation	33.2%	53.12
Information	38.1%	60.96
Service request	12.5%	20.00
Cancellation	9.7%	15.52
Other	6.5%	10.40
TOTAL	100%	160

c. Chi-squared = 5.503, with 4 degrees of freedom.

d. Accept the null hypothesis because the chi-squared statistic (5.503) is smaller than the chi-squared table value (9.488) for testing at the 5% level. Calls for the first day of the month are not significantly different, in the distribution of types of calls, from this month last year.

e. There is no convincing evidence of any change from last year in the distribution of categories of telephone calls. The differences observed could have occurred due to randomness alone.

5. a.

	Managers	Other employees	Total
Better	23	185	208
Same	37	336	373
Worse	11	161	172
Not sure	15	87	102
Total	86	769	855

b. Table of overall percentages:

	Managers	Other Employees	Total
Better	2.69%	21.64%	24.33%
Same	4.33%	39.30%	43.63%
Worse	1.29%	18.83%	20.12%
Not sure	1.75%	10.18%	11.93%
Total	10.06%	89.94%	100%

Each percentage here estimates the probability of the intersection of two events, one event being "managers" or "other employees", and the other event being "better", "same", "worse", or "not sure", where the random experiment refers to a random employee.

The last row estimates the probability of finding a manager (10.06%) or not (89.94%). The last column refers to the probabilities of the four basic responses.

c. Table of percentages by type of employee:

	Managers	Other Employees	Total
Better	26.74%	24.06%	24.33%
Same	43.02%	43.69%	43.63%
Worse	12.79%	20.94%	20.12%
Not sure	17.44%	11.31%	11.93%
Total	100%	100%	100%

The percentages by type of employee show the percentages of "better", "same", "worse", and "not sure" for each type of employee, i.e. for "managers" and for "other employees". For example, to calculate the percentages for managers, you would divide the manager's count for each response by the total number of managers.

The percentages here estimate the conditional probabilities of the responses "better", "same", "worse", and "not sure", GIVEN that the type of employee is "managers" for the first column. Conditional probabilities GIVEN "other employees" are listed in the second column.

The percentages in the last column continue to estimate the unconditional probability of each type of response.

d. Table of percentages by response:

	Managers	Other Employees	Total
Better	11.06%	88.94%	100%
Same	9.92%	90.08%	100%
Worse	6.40%	93.60%	100%
Not sure	14.71%	85.29%	100%
Total	10.06%	89.94%	100%

The percentages in the first column estimate the conditional probabilities of being "managers" GIVEN that the response was "better", "same", "worse", and "not sure" respectively. The percentages in the second column estimate the conditional probabilities of being "other employees" given the response.

The last row estimates the unconditional probability of the event "managers" and of the event "other employees". These are the same percentages which were found in the table of overall percentages.

e.   Yes, they appear to be fairly independent, but not perfectly so. The three columns in the answer to part c are fairly similar to one another (except perhaps for "worse" and "not sure"). Also, note that the five rows in the answer to part d are fairly similar to one another.

7. a.   The critical value is 7.815 at the 5% level, so we accept the null hypothesis because the chi-squared statistic (5.224) is smaller. This indicates that the observed counts are not significantly different from what would be expected if the variables were independent. There is no significant difference in the pattern of responses for managers and for other employees.

b.   The critical value is 11.345 at the 1% level. Accept the null hypothesis.

c.   The critical value is 16.266 at the 0.1% level. Accept the null hypothesis.

d.   There is no significant association between type of employee (manager or not) and opinion as to future business conditions ($p > 0.05$). So far as we can tell based on the individuals sampled, managers and other employees could be in agreement concerning this assessment of the future.

9. a.   In practical terms H_0 claims that stockholders and nonstockholders generally respond in the same way. The null hypothesis claims that the two variables (type of person and response) are independent of one another so that the probability for either variable is equal to the conditional probability given the other variable.

b.   You would expect 44×138/341 = 17.80645. This is the number of stockholders times the number (of everyone) responding "very likely", divided by the total.

c.   Table of expected counts:

	Stockholders	Nonstockholders	Total
Very likely	17.80645	26.19355	44
Somewhat likely	42.89736	63.10264	106
Not very likely	48.56305	71.43695	120
Not likely at all	20.23460	29.76540	50
Not sure	8.49853	12.50147	21
Total	138	203	341

d.   Chi-squared = 0.729.

e.   Degrees of freedom are $(5-1)\times(2-1) = 4$.

11. a.   The order rates are 4.02% (East) and 3.21% (West). The East orders at a higher rate. Don't forget to divide by the total, not by the last row in the given table.

b.   Yes, these order rates are significantly different, based on a chi-squared test of independence (chi-squared = 13.488 with 1 degree of freedom).

13. Yes, the difference is significant, based on a chi-squared test of independence (chi-squared = 15.923 with 1 degree of freedom). This is not likely to have occurred due to random chance alone.

In order to apply chi-squared analysis, you need a table of counts. There is enough information given in the problem to find this table (with two rows and two columns). For example, the number, out of 240 who were asked the "satisfied" question is $0.26\times240 = 62.4$, so you know that this is 62 people.

15. a.   Those in the "satisfied" group (who were asked how satisfied they were) were more likely to report that they were satisfied (either very satisfied or somewhat satisfied), based on the rate of 221/243 = 90.95%, as compared to 197/240 = 82.08% for the "dissatisfied" group.

b.   Those in the "dissatisfied" group were more likely to report being dissatisfied (either somewhat or very dissatisfied), based on rates of 9.05% (for the "satisfied" group) and 17.92% (for the "dissatisfied" group).

c.   Yes, the differences are significant (chi-squared = 8.675 with 3 degrees of freedom). Evidently the way in which the question is asked has a significant impact on the answer.

17. No, your customers do not appear to be special. There are no significant differences between customers and potential customers (chi-squared = 4.444 with 2 degrees of freedom). The observed differences could reasonably have occurred at random.

Chapter 18: Quality Control

Recognizing and Managing Variation

Odd Problem Solutions

1. a.   Pareto diagram. The Pareto diagram displays the problems in the order from most to least frequent so that you can focus attention on the most important problems.

    b.   The R chart. The R chart enables you to monitor the variability of the process, so you can modify it, if that is necessary. This is a variability problem because the engines come out different from one another.

    c.   The $\overline{X}$ chart. The $\overline{X}$ chart displays the average of each sample. This is an average, not a variability, problem because the items are similar to one another but are not the correct size.

    d.   The percentage chart. This chart displays the percent defective together with the central line and control limits, so you can monitor the rate at which the process is producing defective candy coatings.

    e.   The R chart. The R chart monitors the variability of the process, which you hope to understand.

    f.   The percentage chart. This chart monitors the percent of defectives (late-paid bills), and would show if and when things were getting worse.

3. a.

Problem	Cases	Percent	Cumulative Percent
Not enough coating	526	53.3%	53.3%
Squashed	292	29.6%	83.0%
Too much coating	89	9.0%	92.0%
Two stuck together	57	5.8%	97.8%
Miscellaneous	22	2.2%	100.0%
Total	986	100%	

b.

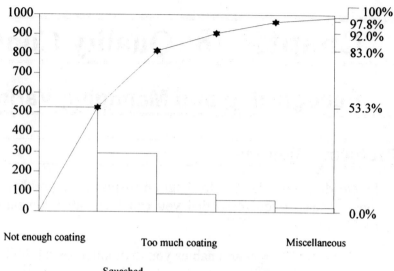

c.   Not enough coating is the most important problem. It represents 53.3% of all difficulties.

d.   "Squashed" is the next most important problem. It represents 29.6% of the total problems.

e.   83.0%.

f.   Exercise for the student. It should emphasize that "not enough coating" and "squashed" are by far the most important problems to fix right away, since together they account for 83.0% of all problems.

5. a.   The chart shows that the average number of chocolate chips stayed within the control limits and close to the center line for the first 23 samples. After that, however, it moved up sharply and crossed the upper control limit.

    b.   This process is not in control because the most recent observations are outside the control limits.

    c.   The process should be interrupted, the cause of the increase in chocolate chips per cookie should be determined, and the problem should be fixed.

7. a.

Sample Number	$\overline{X}$ Average	R Range	Sample Number	$\overline{X}$ Average	R Range
1	12.5933	0.19	14	12.9567	0.23
2	12.5067	0.21	15	12.9767	0.20
3	12.5900	0.41	16	12.9300	0.08
4	12.5367	0.16	17	12.8900	0.26
5	12.6567	0.20	18	12.9567	0.14
6	12.5967	0.32	19	13.0500	0.36
7	12.5733	0.17	20	13.0633	0.20
8	12.5467	0.15	21	12.9300	0.24
9	12.7067	0.24	22	13.0800	0.30
10	12.8400	0.25	23	13.1000	0.05
11	12.8000	0.12	24	13.0900	0.48
12	12.8800	0.08	25	13.1833	0.11
13	13.0233	0.05			

b. $\overline{\overline{X}} = 12.8423$ and $\overline{R} = 0.208$.

c. The center line is 12.8423.

d. The control limits extend from 12.630 to 13.055, which is computed as $\overline{\overline{X}} - A_2\overline{R}$ to $\overline{\overline{X}} + A_2\overline{R}$, where $A_2 = 1.023$.

e.

Averages of Three Measurements

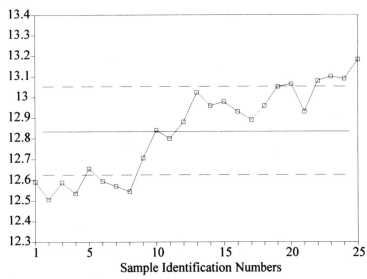

f. This process is not in control. The averages do not stay within the control limits due to an overall upward trend.

g. Exercise for the student. The process is out of control, the protective coating is getting thicker and thicker instead of being stable, and some intervention is necessary to bring the system back in control.

9.   a.

Sample Number	Average	Range	Sample Number	Average	Range
1	8.5050	0.16	11	8.5025	0.15
2	8.4825	0.20	12	8.4775	0.30
3	8.5325	0.33	13	8.5075	0.09
4	8.4600	0.15	14	8.4600	0.19
5	8.5225	0.15	15	8.5625	0.09
6	8.5675	0.18	16	8.4650	0.20
7	8.5475	0.16	17	8.5175	0.16
8	8.4900	0.32	18	8.5650	0.32
9	8.4750	0.26	19	8.5750	0.26
10	8.4550	0.34	20	8.4875	0.38

b. $\overline{\overline{X}} = 8.5079$ and $\overline{R} = 0.2195$.

c.   The center line is $\overline{\overline{X}} = 8.5079$.

d.   The control limits extend from 8.348 to 8.668, which is computed as $\overline{\overline{X}} - A_2\overline{R}$ to $\overline{\overline{X}} + A_2\overline{R}$, where $A_2 = 0.729$.

e.

Average Length

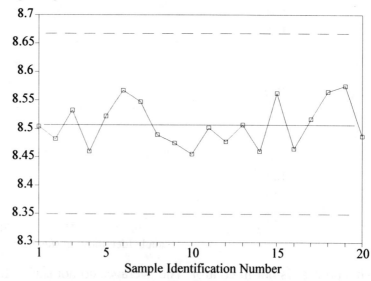

Sample Identification Number

f.   This process is in control. There are no observations outside the control limits. There is no trending which would alert one to a difficulty in the future.

g.   Exercise for the student. The process is in control. No action is necessary beyond a continuation of the current monitoring.

11. a.   Center line = $\bar{p}$ = 0.0731. The control limits extend from 2.80% to 11.82%,

       which is computed as $\bar{p} - 3\sqrt{\dfrac{\bar{p}(1-\bar{p})}{n}}$ to $\bar{p} + 3\sqrt{\dfrac{\bar{p}(1-\bar{p})}{n}}$.

    b.   Center line = $\bar{p}$ = 0.1683. The control limits extend from 11.54% to 22.12%,

       which is computed as $\bar{p} - 3\sqrt{\dfrac{\bar{p}(1-\bar{p})}{n}}$ to $\bar{p} + 3\sqrt{\dfrac{\bar{p}(1-\bar{p})}{n}}$.

    c.   Center line = π_0 = 0.0350. The control limits extend from 1.55% to 5.45%,

       which is computed as $\pi_0 - 3\sqrt{\dfrac{\pi_0(1-\pi_0)}{n}}$ to $\pi_0 + 3\sqrt{\dfrac{\pi_0(1-\pi_0)}{n}}$.

    d.   Center line = π_0 = 0.01. The control limits extend from 0.23% to 1.77%, which

       is computed as $\pi_0 - 3\sqrt{\dfrac{\pi_0(1-\pi_0)}{n}}$ to $\pi_0 + 3\sqrt{\dfrac{\pi_0(1-\pi_0)}{n}}$.

13. a.   Center line = $\bar{p}$ = 8.668%.

    b.   The control limits extend from 6.00% to 11.34%, which is computed as

       $\bar{p} - 3\sqrt{\dfrac{\bar{p}(1-\bar{p})}{n}}$ to $\bar{p} + 3\sqrt{\dfrac{\bar{p}(1-\bar{p})}{n}}$.

    c.

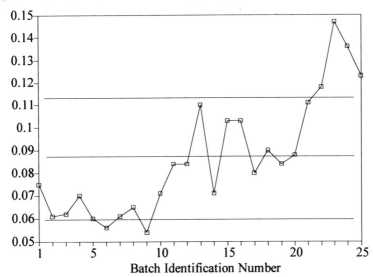

Proportion of Highest Speed Chips

    d.   The process is not in control because there are observations outside the control
       limits. There is also an overall upward trend.

    e.   This is good news. The percentages being charted are the percentages of
       highest-speed chips. Any intervention should be in the direction of finding out
       what is being done right and continuing and extending it.

f.   Exercise for the student. The process is not in control, the efforts to produce more high-speed chips appear to be working.

15. The first observation can fall on either side of the center line - it doesn't matter. After that, however, we are interested in the probability that the remaining 7 observations fall on the same side. Assume that these happen independently of one another and that the probability is 0.5 that a given observation will be on the same side of the center line as the first observation. This is the binomial probability that $X = 7$ where $n = 7$ and $\pi = 0.5$, since we are demanding that all 7 out of 7 happen. Using the formula from the chapter on random variables, the answer is:

$$P(X = 7) = \binom{7}{7} 0.5^7 (1 - 0.5)^{(7-7)} = 1 \times 0.5^7 \times 1 = 0.007813$$

This says that the probability of seeing 8 consecutive points on the same side of the center line, for a process in control, is only 0.007813. Since this happens so rarely for a process in control, when it does happen we reject this null hypothesis and decide that the process is not in control.

17. This process is not in control. The R chart shows one point that is outside the upper control limit, indicating excess variability. Action is needed to bring the variability back under control.

19. This process is not in control. Even though no points are outside the control limits, the $\overline{X}$ chart shows a steady upward trend that is soon likely to go beyond the upper control limit. Action is needed to bring these drifting averages back under control.